The Future of Enterprise Software Delivery:

How AI Is Redefining Enterprise Strategy, Accelerating Software Development, and Delivering Trusted Systems at Scale

By Chris Harasty

Copyright

The Future of Enterprise Software Delivery

ISBN: 978-0-6456052-3-5

First Edition: 2026

For information about permissions, licensing, or bulk purchases, please contact:

Chris Harasty

chris@harasty.com.au

Praise for *The Future of Enterprise Software Delivery*

"This book makes an important and timely contribution to the field of enterprise software delivery. Rather than treating artificial intelligence as a narrow technical innovation, it frames AI as a structural force that reshapes architecture, operating models, governance, and leadership decision-making. The analysis is rigorous, conceptually sound, and grounded in real-world enterprise practice, making it valuable not only for practitioners but also for students and researchers seeking to understand how modern software systems are built and sustained at scale.

What distinguishes this work is its ability to connect theory with execution. The author moves beyond abstract discussion to present a coherent framework that explains why many digital transformation efforts fail and how AI, when combined with disciplined platform engineering and organizational design, can fundamentally improve delivery outcomes. This book would be highly relevant in postgraduate programs in information systems, software engineering, and technology management, and I strongly recommend it to leaders and scholars interested in the future of enterprise systems."

— Professor Marcus Gallagher, University of Queensland

"The most powerful insight in this book is that AI fundamentally changes the cost and speed of enterprise software delivery, but only if organizations redesign their workflows. It reframes AI not as a technology investment, but as a structural advantage when applied with discipline. Highly relevant for all executives focused on ROI."

— Dr Gaurav Srivastava (PhD), CEO, Absolute Vision Technology

This book should be required reading for any senior executive responsible for enterprise technology outcomes. It goes beyond AI hype and clearly explains what must change in business strategy, operating models, and governance for AI to deliver successful projects. It is one of the few books that treats software delivery as a strategic leadership system rather than merely a technological problem."

— Adeeb Khalidch, Enterprise Project Director

"The book stands out for its exceptional use of diagrams to explain complex enterprise software concepts with clarity and precision. As an enterprise architect, I rarely see technical and organizational ideas translated so well into visual models. The diagrams in this book do more than illustrate theory; they provide a useful architectural model for understanding the new processes and governance required for using AI safely."

— Haowei Ruan, Senior Enterprise IT Architect, Global Telco

"Most discussions of AI focus on the massive productivity gains. This book focuses on decision quality, risk, and strategic leverage. It gives boards and senior executives a practical framework for understanding how AI reshapes enterprise software development budgets without sacrificing reliability, compliance, or control. It will greatly assist me in my consulting sales process. I will buy a copy for each of my customers and new prospects."

— Neil Benson, ex-KPMG Partner

"This is the clearest description I have seen of how AI software development requires new work methods. It bridges the gap between technical hype and a practical guide to using the tools sensibly. Our development team has been wondering how use these tools without hallucinations. Now we have a way forward."

— Gary Irwin, CEO, Lava lamp

"Digital transformation has failed many mid-sized organizations because they lack a clear business rationale for their IT projects. The project is led by technology rather than addressing a business need. Using AI without a clear business driver will just make the project worse. The book is helpful because it reframes AI and software development as a business-led discipline, showing C-level executives how to base technology decisions on clear business outcomes and measurable value rather than guesswork."

— Tobi Webster, CEO, Axela

"I enjoyed this book because of its practical treatment of risk in enterprise software projects using the new AI development tools. We work primarily with federal and state government departments, where purchasing decisions are inherently risk-averse. The book describes a methodology that dramatically increases our productivity while also managing project risk. It is essential reading for organizations delivering technology solutions in the regulated public sector."

— Robert Brown, Director, Biz Hub

Dedication

To my wife, Lata, whose love, strength, and unwavering support have carried me through difficult challenges and inspired my ambition. She is the best person I know by far.

I am blessed with four children, whose curiosity, resilience, and energy remind me daily why the future is bright, albeit we live in a world full of political and economic turmoil.

To my family, you are the heart behind everything I create.

Foreword

I began my career in enterprise IT in 1994. Since then, I have worked across large and complex organisations, including Microsoft Consulting Services, and witnessed multiple waves of reform in how software is delivered. Client–server. The early web. SOA. Agile. DevOps. Cloud. Platform engineering.

Each shift improved something. None removed the underlying realities of enterprise delivery.

Enterprise software is constrained by far more than code. It is shaped by governance, regulatory obligation, competing priorities, budget cycles, organisational silos, and legacy systems that cannot simply be replaced. The larger the enterprise, the more accumulated inertia it carries.

For many years, we assumed the primary bottleneck was development throughput. Improve the tools. Refine the process. Increase collaboration. Those were the levers.

Artificial intelligence changes that equation.

AI-assisted development environments can now reason across entire repositories, generate structured code, refactor safely, and produce meaningful test coverage at speeds that would have been inconceivable even a decade ago. The mechanical act of writing software is no longer the dominant constraint.

That shift is significant, and it introduces new responsibility.

Acceleration amplifies whatever system it operates within. If architecture is brittle, if governance is reactive, if ownership is fragmented, AI will surface those weaknesses quickly. Producing software faster does not automatically produce better outcomes.

This is where many organisations will struggle. They will adopt AI tools, expecting transformation while retaining operating models designed for slower cycles. They will increase output without strengthening structure. The result will not be sustained productivity; it will be amplified misalignment.

Harasty's book addresses this directly.

It does not treat AI as a novelty. It treats it as a structural shift that demands corresponding change in architecture, platform engineering, governance, and operating model design. It recognises that durable acceleration requires composable systems, internal developer platforms, embedded security, and disciplined delivery practices.

AI does not remove the need for engineering judgement. It increases the importance of it.

Engineers will spend less time on mechanical implementation and more time on decomposition, architectural coherence, validation, and risk assessment. Leaders will need to rethink how compliance is embedded, how change is governed, and how accountability is structured. Human oversight does not diminish in an AI-augmented environment. It becomes more strategic.

AI tools are powerful. Used well, they compress effort and unlock capacity that enterprises have never had before. Used carelessly, they accelerate technical debt and operational risk just as efficiently.

The difference lies in method.

This book outlines that method. It connects architecture, platform maturity, governance, and AI-enabled workflows into a coherent delivery model. It is not a call to "adopt AI." It is a call to redesign the system that surrounds it.

The future of enterprise software delivery will not be determined by who adopts AI first. It will be determined by who adapts their operating model to support it safely and sustainably.

That distinction matters.

Chris Gibbons
Senior Enterprise Software Architect & Project Director

Preface

Enterprise software delivery has always been shaped by waves of innovation. Each generation introduces new languages, frameworks, deployment models, and architectural patterns that expand what organizations can build. Yet despite these advances, the essential challenge has remained unchanged: delivering high-quality software that meets business needs reliably, repeatedly, and at scale. Over the past several years, however, a deep transformation has begun that is unlike any that preceded it. Artificial intelligence, combined with cloud-native architectures and platform engineering, is fundamentally altering how software is conceived, built, deployed, and governed.

This book was written to help leaders understand and navigate this shift. It is not a catalogue of tools, nor a celebration of technological novelty. Instead, it is an attempt to bring clarity to a landscape defined by rapid change, growing complexity, and extraordinary opportunity. While many organizations sense the importance of AI and automation, far fewer have a clear framework for integrating these capabilities into the core of their engineering and operating models. The objective of this book is to provide that framework.

The idea for this work emerged from conversations with software engineering and business leaders across manufacturing, finance, healthcare, telecommunications, energy, public services, all grappling with similar questions. How will AI reshape software engineering teams? What architectures best support continuous evolution? How do we ensure safety, security, and governance in systems that increasingly adapt themselves? What organizational structures unlock flow rather than restrict it? How do we scale AI software development tools like Cursor responsibly across tens, hundreds, or thousands of developers?

These questions are not simply technical. They reflect a broader shift in the nature of digital-era leadership, where success depends on creating work environments where human and machine intelligence reinforce one another. In studying these challenges, it became clear that enterprises are on the cusp of a new era, one where velocity, adaptability, and autonomous decision-making become defining business-strategic capabilities.

To support this exploration, I have chosen to use diagrams extensively throughout the book. Visual models often distil complex ideas into forms that are easier to understand and apply, making patterns and relationships visible in ways text alone cannot. Wherever a concept benefits from visual clarity, you will find a diagram to reinforce and simplify it.

The book you now hold is the result of exploring that terrain. It combines research from software engineering, AI, organizational theory, and human–computer interaction with practical insights from real-life software development projects. It presents both a strategic lens and an operational guide, suitable for executives, architects, platform teams, and engineering managers seeking to elevate their organizations into the next generation of software delivery.

If this book succeeds, it will help readers not only understand the future but also participate in shaping it. Powerful AI tools are emerging. The principles are becoming clear. The moment for decisive action is now.

Table Of Contents

Executive Summary

Enterprise software delivery is undergoing a fundamental transformation driven by advances in artificial intelligence, platform engineering, and cloud-native architectures. For the first time, organizations can combine human expertise with machine intelligence to create software systems that evolve continuously, operate with unprecedented reliability, and support strategic decision-making at every level. This book presents a comprehensive framework for understanding and navigating this shift.

Modern enterprises face rising complexity, continuously increasing demand for digital capabilities, and intense pressure to innovate faster. Traditional software delivery models, characterized by siloed teams, manual workflows, and brittle legacy architectures, cannot keep pace with these expectations. The emergence of AI-augmented software development environments marks a structural break from these limitations. Modern tools like Cursor.com can analyze entire code repositories, reason across complex codebases, generate tests, and accelerate refactoring with remarkable effectiveness. Cursor is referenced as a practical example because, at the time of writing, it represented the most mature AI-enabled development environment, while the principles discussed remain tool-agnostic and applicable to other platforms. Research consistently demonstrates that when used within structured workflows and supported by appropriate governance, AI can dramatically increase developer productivity, reduce cognitive load, and improve software quality.

However, the benefits of AI cannot be realized in isolation. AI-driven development flourishes only when built on stable architectural foundations and mature platform capabilities. Internal Developer Platforms provide the standardization, automation, and guardrails necessary for high-velocity change. These platforms offer secure and governed pathways for provisioning, deployment, observability, and compliance, enabling teams to deliver software safely and consistently. By reducing human cognitive overhead and enforcing architectural patterns, they create an environment in which AI-generated contributions can be integrated reliably at scale.

As software systems become more modular, more distributed, and more intelligent, security and governance require corresponding evolution. Traditional point-in-time checks are inadequate for environments defined by continuous deployment, automated code generation, and dynamic infrastructure. Organizations must adopt real-time, policy-as-code approaches capable of continuously validating behavior across every layer of the stack. This transformation brings security closer to development workflows and makes compliance an automated property of the system rather than a periodic event.

The shift toward AI-augmented engineering also transforms the composition and capabilities of software teams. Software engineers increasingly collaborate with AI systems, directing their efforts through decomposition, verification, iterative refinement, and architectural reasoning. Their role becomes more strategic and conceptual as machines assume a greater share of repetitive, mechanical work. Organizations benefit most when they cultivate hybrid teams where humans and AI systems complement each other's strengths. Studies in human-AI collaboration confirm that such teams consistently outperform those relying solely on human effort or automation.

To support this new way of working, enterprises must adopt operating models designed for speed, autonomy, and continuous learning. Domain-aligned, long-lived product teams outperform project-oriented structures. Continuous decision-making replaces periodic planning, and experimentation becomes a core organizational capability. Leadership needs to shift from controlling change to enabling it, fostering cultures where teams are empowered to innovate within well-defined boundaries.

This book also provides practical guidance for implementing AI-enhanced development environments. It outlines strategies for adopting powerful AI software development tools safely and effectively. We identify patterns that increase accuracy and reliability and describe anti-patterns that heighten risk. It presents training pathways to equip teams with the skills required for AI-augmented software development, and it details the governance mechanisms necessary for responsible adoption. Finally, it provides a vision of the enterprise of the future, an organization defined by adaptive systems, intelligent platforms, hybrid teams, and continuous innovation.

In summary, the future of enterprise software delivery will be shaped by those who embrace AI not as a tool to automate existing processes, but as a catalyst for reimagining how software is built, maintained, and evolved. The enterprises that succeed will be those that modernize their architectures, invest in platform engineering, redesign their operating models, build new forms of organizational capability, and cultivate teams prepared to work in partnership with intelligent systems. The strategic advantage will belong to those who recognize that the era ahead is not simply about writing code faster, but about building smarter, more adaptive, and more resilient organizations.

Introduction

Enterprise software delivery is undergoing a profound and irreversible transformation. Over the past decade, organizations have steadily modernized through cloud adoption, DevOps practices, microservices architectures, and continuous integration pipelines. Yet these advances, significant as they are, constitute only a prelude to a far larger shift now reshaping the nature of software itself. Artificial intelligence, platform engineering, and composable architectures are converging to create a fundamentally new model of software delivery. One that is faster, more adaptive, more autonomous, and more deeply integrated with business strategy. AI-based software development frameworks based on Machine Learning (ML), Natural Language Processing (NLP), and deep neural networks automate software system design and coding. The framework is fully integrated into development environments, allowing for real-time pattern suggestions, adaptive code refactoring, and automatic code generation. AI tools can "understand" source code, detect anti-patterns, and suggest the best possible design components, yielding improvements in accuracy, productivity, and code quality. This framework facilitates automated decision-making in repetitive design areas, integrating AI into the architectural process and leading to the creation of innovative smart tools. It highlights how AI has the potential to transform the principles of software architecture, enabling accelerated innovation and practical systems for maintenance [1].

This book takes as its central premise that enterprise software delivery is entering an era defined not by incremental improvements but by significant structural change. Advanced AI-enabled development environments, such as Cursor, are not merely tools that enhance productivity;

they represent a new cognitive layer within the software engineering process.

In this book, Cursor is referenced solely as a practical example because, at the time of writing, it represented a mature AI-enabled development environment. This reference does not constitute a recommendation, and the principles discussed are intentionally tool-agnostic and applicable across current and future platforms.

These AI tools can analyze entire repositories, reason across codebases, propose architectural transformations, and execute complex refactoring at speeds unattainable by human effort alone. As a result, the act of building software is shifting from manual construction toward a partnership between human expertise and machine intelligence. Integration of cognitive models with AI-driven code generation improves software development by optimizing code generation, refactoring code, and repairing defects. This system demonstrates faster performance and reduced complexity compared to human-written code, leading to shorter task completion times and fewer errors for developers [2]. Early studies already indicate that this hybrid model significantly improves velocity, quality, and developer experience, provided that it is implemented with clear governance and technical discipline [3],[4],[5],[6].

Alongside these cognitive advances, enterprises are adopting platform engineering as a structural foundation for high-velocity software delivery. Internal Developer Platforms increasingly serve as the connective tissue of modern organizations, supplying consistent workflows, secure deployment paths, and governed integration points for distributed teams. These platforms dramatically reduce cognitive load, create coherence across diverse systems, and provide the guardrails necessary for safe and scalable AI augmentation.

Research shows that organizations that pair AI-enabled development with mature platform practices achieve disproportionate gains in efficiency, reliability, and product flow yet technology alone is not sufficient [7]. The shift toward intelligent, continuously evolving systems requires corresponding changes in organizational structure, talent models, and leadership philosophy. While AI adoption promises benefits such as enhanced efficiency, productivity, and innovation, it also presents significant challenges, including cultural alignment, employee resistance, ethical concerns, and challenges in leadership communication. Effective leadership, transparent communication, and investments in skills development emerge as pivotal strategies for overcoming these obstacles and ensuring successful AI implementation. Engineers must learn to collaborate with AI systems, guiding them through decomposition, verification, refactoring, and architectural reasoning. Leaders must evolve operating models to support domain-aligned teams, rapid decision cycles, and cultures of experimentation. Governance models must adapt to ensure security, compliance, and responsible AI behavior. Human and machine roles must become complementary rather than adversarial, with each contributing its strengths to create higher-order capabilities than either could achieve independently [8].

This book examines these transformations in depth, offering both a conceptual framework and a practical guide for leaders navigating the future of enterprise software delivery. The chapters that follow explore the evolution of architectures, the rise of platform engineering, the redefinition of security and governance in an AI-driven world, and the emergence of hybrid human–AI development practices. They also include detailed chapters outlining implementation strategies for Cursor, design patterns for AI-augmented engineering, and governance considerations for safe and effective adoption.

The purpose of this work is twofold. First, it seeks to provide clarity about the technological and organizational forces reshaping modern software delivery, grounding its analysis in research, empirical evidence, and industry best practice. Second, it serves as a roadmap for transformation, helping enterprises build the capabilities, structures, and cultures required to compete in an environment where adaptability, intelligence, and velocity are the defining business strategic assets.

The audience for this book includes technology executives, engineering leaders, enterprise architects, platform teams, transformation officers, and senior developers. Whether the reader is guiding a large-scale digital transformation or designing the next generation of enterprise systems, the insights in this book aim to support informed, strategic, and future-ready decision-making.

The future of enterprise software delivery is already emerging. It is a future in which systems evolve continuously, developers work alongside intelligent agents, platforms orchestrate complexity at scale, and organizations innovate with unprecedented speed. This book invites readers to understand that future, prepare for it, and ultimately shape it.

Chapter 1

The New Era of Enterprise Software Delivery

Enterprise software delivery is undergoing its most significant transformation since the introduction of Agile and DevOps. This shift is structural rather than cyclical, driven by rising customer expectations, persistent economic pressure, and rapid advancements in cloud and artificial intelligence technologies. Empirical research consistently shows that organizations with strong software delivery performance excel on deployment frequency, lead time, reliability, and organizational outcomes [9], [10], [11]. In this environment, software is no longer a back-office function; it is a primary driver of value creation, customer experience, and competitive differentiation.

Incremental improvements are no longer adequate. Studies in continuous software engineering show that high-performing organizations integrate development, operations, and feedback loops into cohesive, data-driven workflows rather than treating them as isolated phases [12], [13]. Modern enterprises rely on software to drive revenue, manage risk, coordinate operations, deliver personalized customer experiences, and shape their strategic posture. This new era demands delivery capabilities that are adaptive, automated, intelligent, and capable of coordinating both human and AI-driven contributions. Traditional software delivery models with long lead times, manual workflows, and rigid organizational boundaries cannot support the pace, complexity, and risk profile of contemporary digital-first enterprises.

1.1 The Strategic Shift Driving Modern Delivery

Over the past two decades, enterprises adopted Agile, DevOps, and cloud transformation to accelerate delivery. Systematic reviews of DevOps practices show measurable gains in deployment frequency, lead time for change, reliability, and team performance, especially when automation and cultural alignment are present [14], [15], [16]. Yet even mature DevOps organizations are hitting diminishing returns due to fragmented tooling, architectural sprawl, and expanding and conflicting governance requirements.

Industry-wide performance expectations have shifted dramatically. The DevOps Research and Assessment (DORA) group demonstrates that elite performers deploy multiple times per day with lower change failure rates and faster incident recovery than slower organizations [10], [11]. These findings have been validated across years and industries, making the DORA metrics the de facto standard for measuring software delivery effectiveness.

Customers also expect digital systems to improve continuously without disruption. Research in continuous delivery shows a direct correlation between rapid release cycles and customer satisfaction, business agility, and innovation capacity [13], [17]. Digital-native competitors, architected for speed and experimentation, demonstrate that rapid delivery and high quality are mutually reinforcing rather than mutually exclusive.

Enterprises face a dual mandate: accelerate software delivery while strengthening quality, governance, and security. Meeting this mandate requires a fundamental shift in operating models, toolchains, and architectural patterns

1.2 The Enterprise Software Delivery Landscape: Past Versus Present

Enterprise software delivery historically evolved across three paradigms: Waterfall, Agile, and DevOps. Each attempted to address deficiencies in the previous one.

Waterfall emphasized predictability but lacked adaptability. Agile introduced iterative delivery, customer collaboration, and rapid feedback, but often struggled to scale across complex organizational structures. DevOps integrated development and operations, emphasizing automation, shared ownership, and CI/CD practices. Multiple studies confirm that DevOps improves deployment speed, reliability, and team efficiency [14], [15], [16].

However, DevOps remains heavily dependent on human coordination. Automation exists, but it is procedural rather than intelligent. It requires scripts, pipelines, and configuration files triggered by human judgment. As systems grow more heterogeneous and distributed, cognitive load increases significantly. Continuous software engineering research demonstrates that architectural and tooling complexity directly amplifies cognitive burden, reducing developer throughput and increasing defect rates [13], [17].

Modern enterprises need architectural strategies that reduce unnecessary coupling, delivery platforms that abstract underlying complexity, and intelligent systems that participate actively in engineering work rather than simply providing static automation. Figure 1.1 shows the evolution from linear delivery to iterative, automated, and finally intelligent ways of working. It highlights how each stage builds on the last: Waterfall to Agile to DevOps, culminating in the emerging era of Intelligent Delivery, where speed, feedback loops, and autonomy are significantly amplified.

Figure 1.1 The Evolution of Enterprise Delivery Paradigms

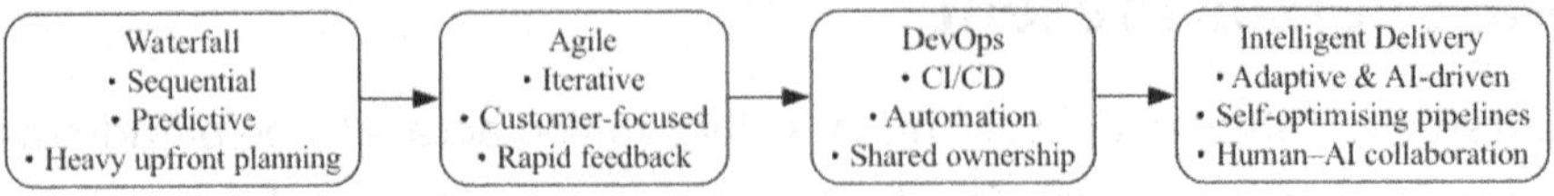

1.3 Market Forces Transforming Enterprise IT

Four structural forces are accelerating the transformation of enterprise software delivery:

1. Cloud Maturity and Multi-Cloud Expansion

Cloud-native architectures built on microservices, containers, and serverless functions have become standard. Microservices enable optimized load balancing, allowing individual services to scale independently based on demand, reducing the strain on system resources and ensuring higher availability and responsiveness. Efficiency gains from microservices are particularly noticeable in terms of development speed, fault isolation, and resource utilization [18]. Surveys and mapping studies highlight the benefits of microservices, scalability, resilience, and decentralized development, as well as the operational challenges associated with distributed systems [19]. Multi-cloud adoption amplifies this complexity, making consistent delivery automation essential.

2. Proliferation of SaaS and Shadow IT

Business units increasingly adopt specialized SaaS tools, creating fragmented architectures. Integration, security, compliance, and governance challenges intensify, requiring platform-centric approaches and more sophisticated lifecycle automation.

3. Economic Pressure and Talent Scarcity

The demand for software capability continues to exceed global talent supply. High-performing DevOps organizations achieve more with less by reducing rework, shortening feedback loops, and automating manual tasks [9], [11], [20]. Automation and AI are becoming necessary to close capability gaps and maintain competitiveness under budget constraints.

4. Rapid Adoption of AI Across the Software Lifecycle

AI has matured into a core enabler of software engineering productivity. Controlled studies of AI-assisted development tools, particularly large language model (LLM) powered code generation, show significant reductions in task completion time and increases in perceived productivity, quality, and workflow satisfaction [16], [21], [22], [23].

AI's impact depends on the organizational context, tooling integration, and the maturity of the business delivery system. AI's transformative potential is merely one aspect of a larger transformation. As depicted in Figure 1.2, it is crucial to consider it alongside other structural factors that are changing enterprise software delivery to properly contextualize its role.

Figure 1.2 Structural Forces Reshaping Enterprise Software Delivery

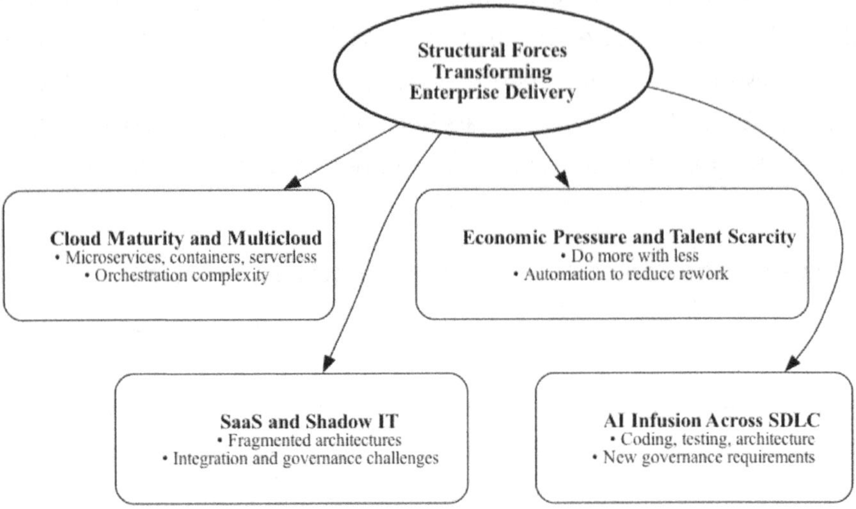

1.4 The Rise of Intelligent, Automated Delivery

The most transformative development in software delivery is the rise of AI systems that not only automate routine tasks but also participate intelligently in engineering work. AI copilots can generate code, propose refactoring strategies, write documentation, and produce targeted test suites. Architectural reasoning tools can detect dependency issues, drift, and deviations from preferred patterns. AI-enabled observability systems can predict incidents, isolate root causes, and trigger proactive remediation.

Studies on AI-driven development highlight three major benefits:

1. Faster completion of routine engineering tasks [24], [25].
2. Increased consistency and standardization across codebases [23].
3. Lower cognitive load and improved flow for developers [22].

The organization achieves step-change results through the combined impact of these benefits. Figure 1.3 summarizes this value chain, showing how better quality, increased developer efficiency, faster delivery, and ongoing improvement are enabled by rapid feedback loops and AI support.

Figure 1.3 Benefits of AI-Augmented Software Delivery

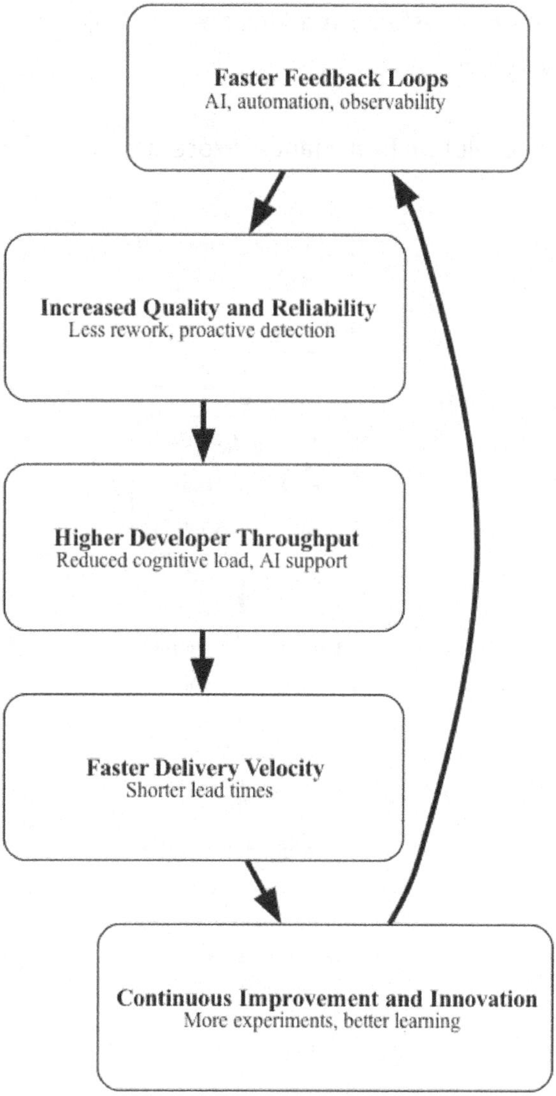

Combined with continuous integration and continuous delivery (CI/CD) pipelines, these capabilities push delivery environments toward **adaptive automation**, automated systems that evaluate context, apply policy, and learn from ongoing activity. Figure 1.4 below shows how modern software delivery is moving from human-led oversight to intelligent, self-optimizing systems, marking the core trajectory of today's software delivery model.

Figure 1.4 The Evolution from Manual Processes to Adaptive Systems

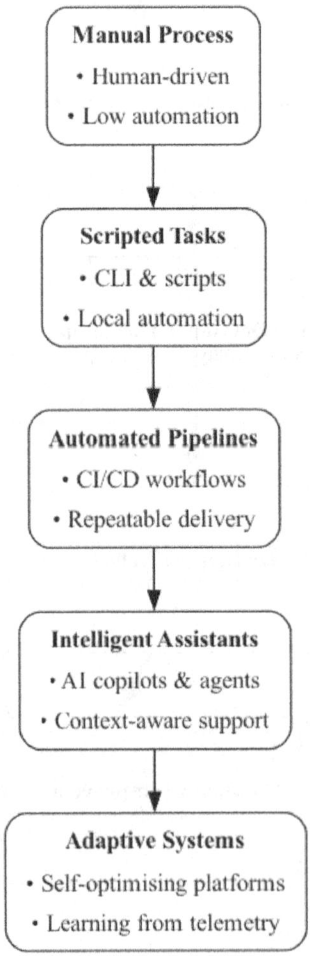

This evolution elevates, rather than replaces, engineering roles. Human judgment will increasingly focus on system design, domain architecture, oversight, ethical constraints, and evaluation of machine outputs. This new partnership requires a clear separation of cognitive responsibilities. Figure 1.5 outlines the complementary strengths of people and AI: humans provide strategy, design, and ethical governance, while AI handles execution and pattern recognition.

Figure 1.5 The Division of Labor in AI-Augmented Engineering

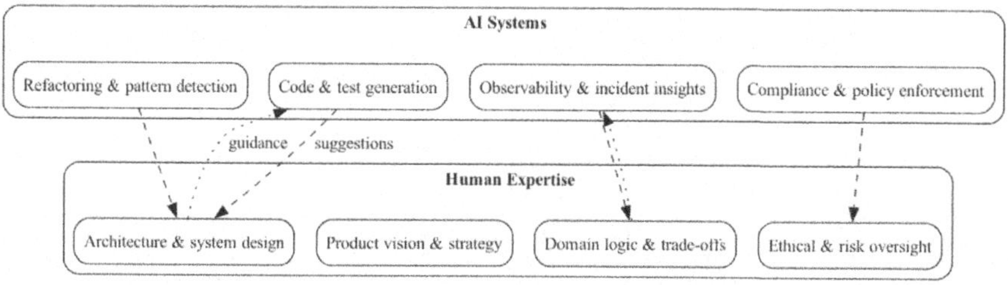

1.5 The Vision for the Next Decade

The next decade will be defined by organizations that successfully integrate:

1. AI-augmented engineering teams
   that use AI to amplify capacity, reduce toil, and accelerate high-quality delivery [22], [24], [25].
2. Composable, cloud-native architectures
   that reduce coupling, support continuous change, and scale more gracefully than monolithic systems [19], [26].
3. Platform engineering and internal developer platforms
   that provide standardized, self-service workflows, golden paths, and governance enforcement at scale [14], [27].

These three pillars, platform engineering, composable architecture, and AI-augmented teams, come together to form a unified operating model. Figure 1.6 illustrates this stack, showing how cloud-native design, automation platforms, intelligent workflows, and a secure, encrypted foundation work together to deliver business outcomes.

Figure 1.6 The Intelligent Delivery Operating Model Stack

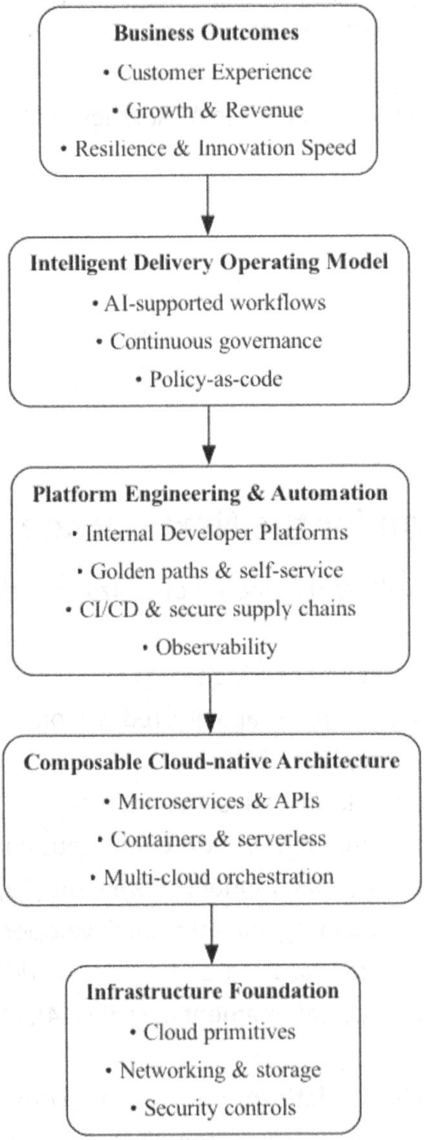

These organizations will deliver software faster, more reliably, and at a lower marginal cost per change. The goal of connecting these three pillars (Figure 1.7) is to move teams out of complex, high cognitive-load work and into controlled simplicity, where platforms and automated processes create focus and flow. Software will increasingly function like a living system, continuously adapting, improving, self-optimizing, and evolving through a blend of human and machine intelligence.

Figure 1.7 The Target State: Reducing Complexity and Cognitive Load through Platform Intelligence

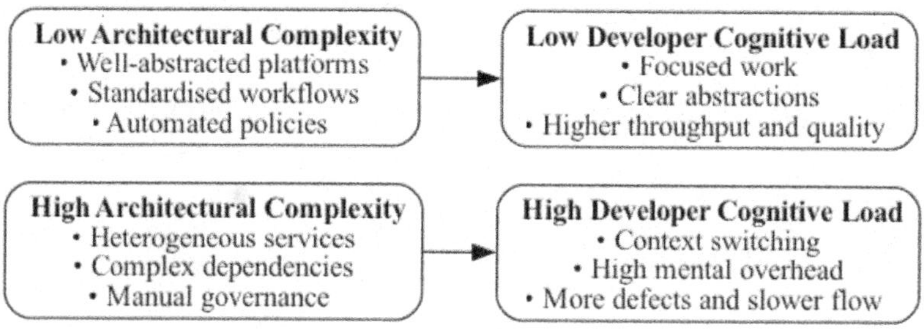

The chapters that follow will examine these themes in depth, outlining the architectures, operating models, AI technologies, and governance patterns that define the future of enterprise software delivery.

Chapter 2

Cloud-Native Architecture and the Rise of Composable Systems

Modern enterprises operate in an environment defined by continuous change. Customer expectations evolve rapidly, competitive threats emerge unexpectedly, and digital channels create unrelenting demand for seamless, always-on services. In this operating reality, the ability to adapt, to create, modify, and deploy software capabilities quickly and safely has become a decisive organizational competency. Cloud-native and composable architectures are at the center of this digital transformation.

Across the last decade, cloud-native principles have moved from experimental engineering practices to become a foundational enterprise strategy. Organizations increasingly view architecture not as a technical blueprint but as a business enabler: a structural mechanism that determines speed, resilience, cost efficiency, and the ability to innovate. Research emphasizes that the architecture of an organization's systems is one of the strongest predictors of delivery performance, scalability, and organizational agility. Integrating well-architected principles into cloud-native architectures is not merely a technical exercise but a strategic necessity. It empowers organizations to build systems that are robust against adversity, secure by design, and efficient in operation. This commitment to resilience does more than just prevent violations; it cultivates an environment of agility and innovation, allowing businesses to adapt swiftly to market changes. By championing these principles, companies can ensure their cloud implementations are not only strong and reliable but also powerful enablers of long-term strategic business goals [20], [28].

Composable systems build on this foundation by allowing enterprises to assemble digital capabilities, applications, services, processes, and data flows like Lego building blocks. Rather than crafting large, tightly coupled systems, organizations create modular, interchangeable components that can be independently evolved, replaced, or scaled. This modularity delivers strategic flexibility that traditional monolithic systems fundamentally cannot provide.

This chapter examines the strategic rationale behind cloud-native and composable architectures, why they have become essential to modern enterprise operations, and how they reshape governance, economics, and organizational structure. This change is part of a broader evolution in how organizations deliver software. Figure 2.1 illustrates the journey from traditional Waterfall approaches to today's modern practices, showing how Agile, DevOps, and AI-augmented engineering build on one another to increase autonomy, speed, and the quality of feedback loops. It also asserts that small, incremental tweaks are not enough: the shift requires a structural move from manual, sequential processes to automated, collaborative systems.

Figure 2.1 Evolution of Enterprise Software Delivery Paradigms

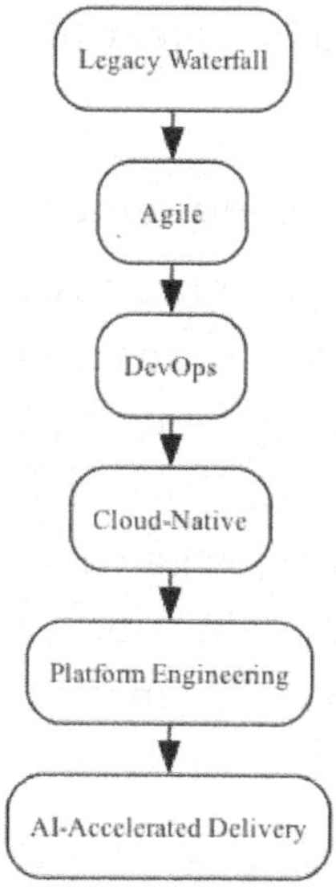

2.1 The Strategic Imperative for Cloud-Native Adoption

The transition to cloud-native architecture is not merely a technology refresh. It represents a shift in enterprise operating principles, from static infrastructure and linear release cycles to dynamic systems that evolve continuously. Several strategic imperatives drive this transition:

Faster Time to Market

Cloud-native systems reduce the friction associated with provisioning environments, integrating new components, and deploying changes. Research shows that organizations adopting microservices and container orchestration significantly reduce deployment lead times and accelerate iterative delivery [19], [20].

For enterprises competing in markets defined by digital acceleration, the ability to deliver software weekly, or even daily has moved from a competitive advantage to a basic requirement.

Resilience as a Business Requirement

Traditional architectures concentrate risk: a single failure can degrade entire systems. Cloud-native architectures distribute functionality across independent services, isolating faults and improving overall resilience. Studies related to microservice architectures highlight improved fault tolerance and service continuity compared with monolithic systems[20]. This resilience is not just technical; it directly impacts customer experience, brand trust, and regulatory compliance.

Elasticity and Cost Alignment

Cloud-native architectures exploit elastic infrastructure: systems can scale automatically based on real-time demand. This should reduce the over-provisioning of IT resources and capital expenditure typical of on-premises deployments. However, the improved cost efficiency is somewhat offset by the ever-increasing costs of advanced cloud services from the major cloud vendors. Empirical and industry research show that elasticity, combined with usage-based pricing, creates more predictable cost structures and aligns expenditure with value creation [29].

Enabling Continuous Innovation

As cloud-native systems are modular, developers can test new ideas without risking core system stability. Teams can safely experiment, iterate, and deploy improvements continuously. This capacity for rapid experimentation is a foundational capability in modern digital enterprises.

2.2 From Monolithic to Modular: Why Composability Matters

The shift toward composable architectures extends the cloud-native paradigm beyond technology into business design. Composable architecture refers to the creation of systems assembled from modular, autonomous components, often called Packaged Business Capabilities (PBCs).

Structural Agility Through Modularization

Research emphasizes that modular system design is strongly correlated with organizational agility and adaptability [6], [28]. When systems are modular:

- New features can be added without large-scale system rewrites.
- Teams can operate autonomously, reducing dependencies and handoffs.
- Upgrades and replacements become easier and less risky.

Instead of relying on a single, centralized codebase, enterprises can evolve capabilities at different speeds depending on business priority.

Reducing Complexity by Designing for Change

Monolithic architectures accumulate complexity over time: dependencies multiply, knowledge centralizes, and the cost of change increases. Composable architectures reduce structural complexity by separating responsibilities and making boundaries explicit.

This aligns system design with business process design. Each PBC reflects a business domain. For example, payments, onboarding, pricing, and identity can be independently evolved by the teams that own those domains.

Strategic Vendor Flexibility

Composable systems reduce vendor lock-in. When capabilities are modular, enterprises can replace third-party components with minimal disruption. This flexibility improves negotiation power, reduces long-term risk, and enables the adoption of best-in-class solutions as markets evolve.

A Foundation for AI Integration

AI capabilities integrate more effectively into modular systems, where data flows and component boundaries are well defined. Composable architectures enable AI-driven automation, dynamic routing, and real-time decision making. These factors form the core capabilities for next-generation enterprise systems. Composable architectures, combined with intelligent workflow automation, further accelerate the push to faster time-to-market. Figure 2.2 highlights AI's role in decision-making, showing how modular design enables intelligent automation and optimization. It also presents an AI-driven approach to backlog prioritization, where machine learning assesses signals such as business value and customer feedback. This shifts organizations from project-based planning to continuous value-based decision-making, improving alignment and coordination around the highest-impact outcomes.

Figure 2.2 AI-Driven Backlog Prioritization

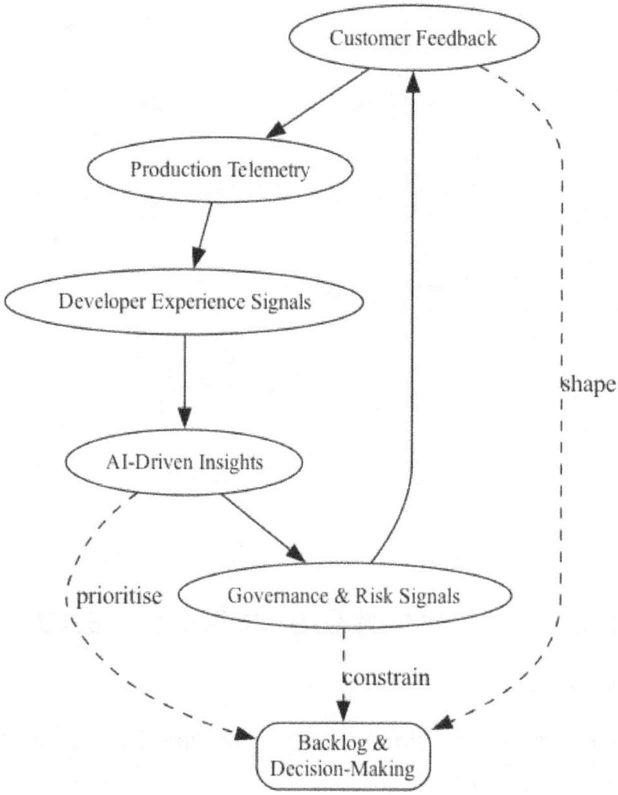

A practical way to understand this modular approach is to look at how it is expressed in architecture. Figure 2.3 presents a modern Enterprise Value Stream, highlighting how an AI and automation layer can be embedded within a traditional delivery model to lift efficiency and improve decision-making. By strengthening platform capabilities and the delivery pipeline, AI helps accelerate the move from strategy to execution. In today's organizations, data intelligence and automation are critical at every stage of the product lifecycle. This layered model reinforces that composability is both an organizational strategy and a technical pattern, enabling independent scaling, faster change, and flexible service delivery across distributed teams.

Figure 2.3 The Composable Enterprise Stack

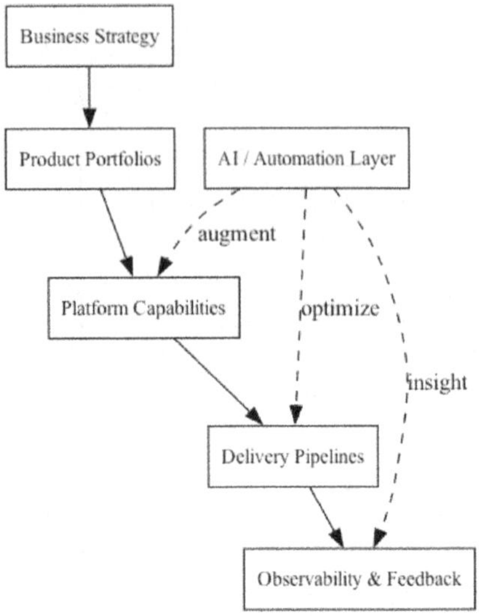

2.3 The Economics of Cloud-Native and Composable Systems

Enterprise leaders increasingly evaluate architecture through the lens of economics: velocity, efficiency, risk reduction, and long-term cost structure.

Lower Cost of Change

With modular architectures, teams can make targeted changes without triggering full-system deployments or extensive regression testing. Studies indicate this significantly lowers the marginal cost of change and increases overall development throughput [6], [20]. These efficiencies are reflected in how teams spend their time. Figure 2.4 compares legacy delivery with AI-enabled delivery, showing less time spent on maintenance and more on value creation.

Figure 2.4 Time Allocation: Legacy vs. Modern Delivery

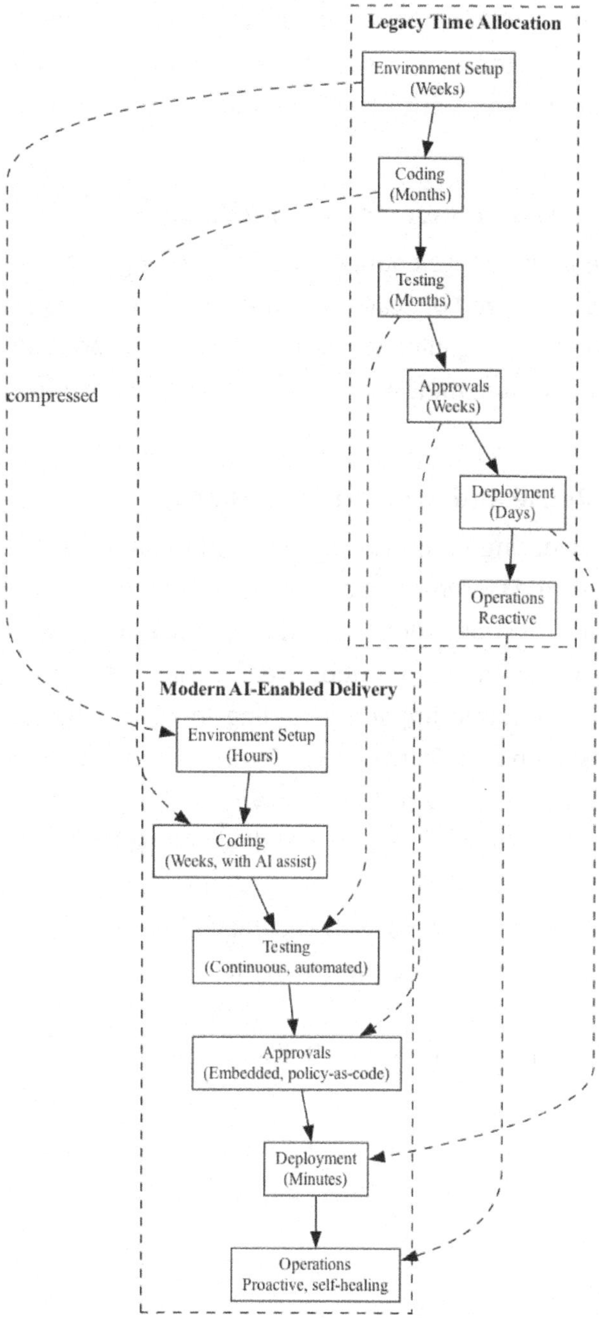

Reduced Operational Overhead Through Automation

Cloud-native platforms automate provisioning, scaling, logging, security patching, and failover, reducing manual workload and operational head-count. Platform automation also reduces the frequency of human-caused incidents, a major contributor to downtime.

Better Alignment of Investment and Value

Composable architecture enables targeted funding: high-value capabilities can be modernized or scaled without investing in large, system-wide upgrades. This is a significant improvement over traditional enterprise platforms that require multiyear, multimillion-dollar rewrites.

Increased Reuse and Avoided Redundancy

Enterprises adopting composable architectures often see major reductions in duplicated systems and processes. Rather than each business unit commissioning bespoke tools, shared PBCs provide consistent, reusable capabilities across the organization. Teams then use delivery metrics to quantify the economic impact, including lower change costs and improved operational effectiveness. Figure 2.5 summarizes the key measures of high-velocity software delivery, linking architectural choices to lead time, deployment frequency, and reliability. These metrics capture more than technical efficiency; they also correlate with customer retention, market responsiveness, and organizational resilience, providing a clear framework for ongoing improvement.

Figure 2.5 Key Metrics for Modern Delivery Flow

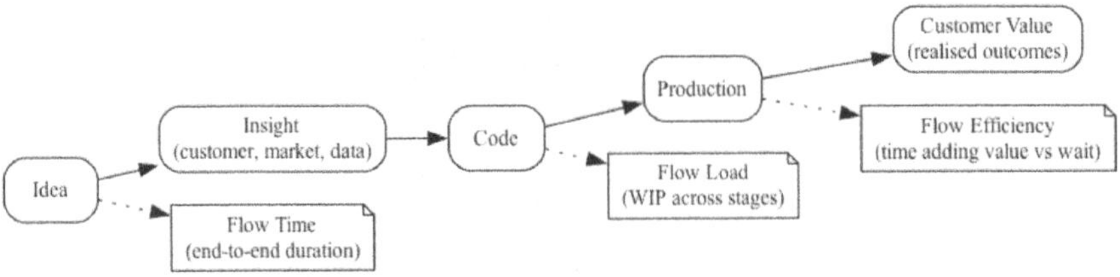

2.4 Governance, Compliance, and Risk Management in Composable Enterprises

As enterprises adopt cloud-native and composable architectures, governance models must evolve accordingly.

Policy as Architecture

Governance is increasingly implemented through architectural choices rather than documentation. For example:

- Security controls are embedded into platform templates.
- Compliance requirements are automatically validated in CI/CD pipelines.
- Observability and auditability are standardized at the platform layer.

This reflects the broader move toward platform engineering and policy-as-code highlighted in contemporary DevOps research[30]. Rather than relying on manual oversight, governance is embedded directly into the platform and delivery pipelines, as illustrated in Figure 2.6. The figure shows security, compliance, and policy enforcement operating continuously across modular components. This approach enables organizations to maintain safety and regulatory compliance at scale without sacrificing delivery speed, and it aligns with zero-trust principles.

Figure 2.6 Automated Governance in a Composable System

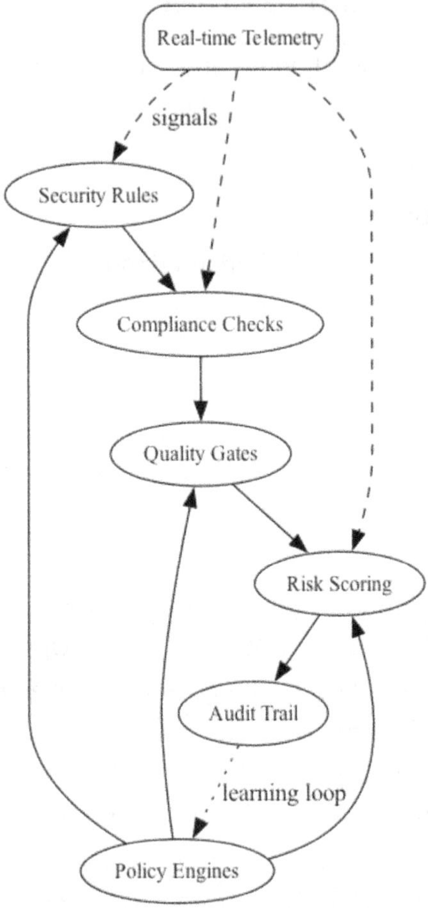

Reducing Systemic Risk Through Decoupling

Modular architectures inherently reduce systemic risk: failures are contained within individual components rather than cascading across monolithic systems. From a governance perspective, this creates more predictable failure domains and faster mean time to recovery.

Improved Transparency and Auditability

Composable architectures produce richer metadata, component boundaries, APIs, contracts, and dependency relationships, which improve auditability and simplify regulatory reporting. Automated evidence collection in CI/CD pipelines further reduces the compliance burden.

Supporting Zero Trust and Modern Security Models

Cloud-native environments are naturally suited to zero-trust practices, including identity-based security, fine-grained policy controls, and continuous verification. Research notes that in distributed architectures, security must be applied at every service boundary rather than managed through a single central point [31]. To support this shift toward platform engineering and product-aligned teams, organizations need a technical foundation that enables autonomy at scale. Figure 2.7 outlines the structure of an internal developer platform, showing how platform teams equip product teams with standardized services and "golden paths" while maintaining governance and consistency.

Figure 2.7 Platform Engineering Architecture

2.5 Organizational and Operating Model Implications

The transition to cloud-native and composable systems is as much organizational as it is technical.

Moving from Project Teams to Product Teams

Composable enterprises organize teams around PBCs and long-lived teams with end-to-end ownership of a discrete business capability. This increases accountability, reduces cross-team dependencies, and accelerates delivery.

The Rise of Platform Engineering

Platform engineering teams build and maintain internal developer platforms that provide golden paths for building, deploying, and operating cloud-native systems. This approach standardizes best practices while allowing product teams autonomy. Platforms become strategic assets rather than technical utilities. Building platform engineering as a strategic DevOps skill underscores the importance of giving robust, effective, and developer-friendly software delivery ecosystems top priority. For teams using IDPs in modern, cloud-native environments, it serves as an organizational and technical manual [32].

Upskilling and Talent Evolution

Architects and engineers must learn new skills:

- distributed system design
- API and event-driven thinking
- cloud infrastructure management
- automated governance and security

Business leaders also need to recognise that architecture is a strategic capability closely tied to competitive advantage. Together, technical expertise, platform engineering, and intelligence capabilities form a new enterprise delivery model. Figure 2.8 presents this integrated framework, showing how platform engineering, cloud-native architecture, and AI-augmented development operate as interdependent pillars that enable organizational agility and sustained innovation.

Figure 2.8 The Three Pillars of Modern Delivery

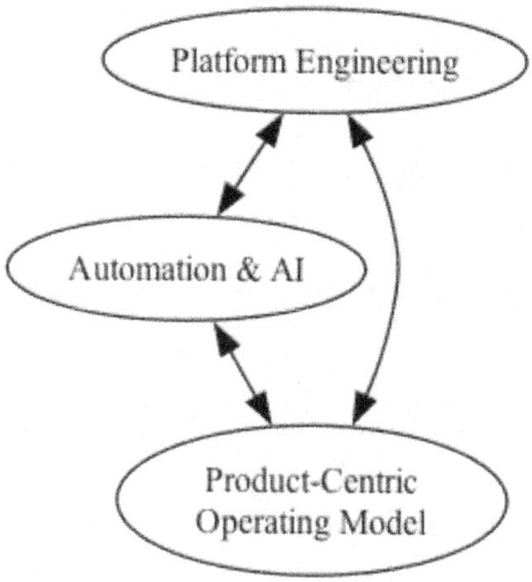

Cultural Shift Toward Autonomy and Accountability

Composable architecture depends on teams taking clear ownership of the components they create. This cultural shift enables innovation, reduces bottlenecks, and reinforces continuous improvement. AI's integration across the entire delivery lifecycle underpins this future of intelligence and adaptation. Figure 2.9 illustrates the AI-augmented approach, showing how machine intelligence applied throughout design, coding, testing, deployment, and operations enables the dynamic, continuously evolving systems that define modern enterprises.

Figure 2.9 AI-Augmented Software Delivery Lifecycle

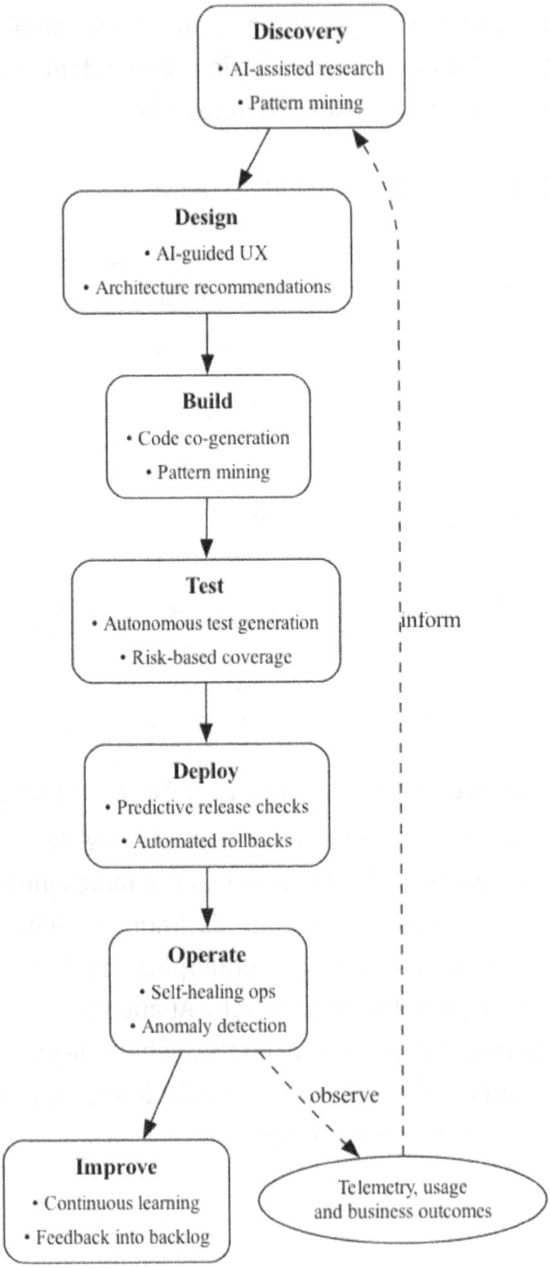

2.6 The Strategic Future of Cloud-Native and Composable Enterprises

As enterprises mature in cloud-native and composable practices, they move toward what Gartner refers to as the "Composable Enterprise", an organization able to reconfigure itself in response to market change. Research and industry analysis suggest that enterprises that master composability will enjoy:

- Faster adaptation to new business models
- Improved resilience during market disruptions
- Significantly lower long-term technology debt
- Greater ability to integrate AI and automation
- More predictable and efficient cost structures

In summary, composable architecture is not just a technology choice; it is a business strategy. It enables organizations to operate with structural agility, simplify complexity, innovate more quickly, and adapt to shifting conditions.

As software increasingly becomes the vehicle through which enterprises execute strategy, the architecture behind that software becomes a key driver of competitive advantage. To translate this ambition into a practical roadmap, organizations must first assess their current capabilities. Figure 2.10 provides a forward-looking framework to help leaders identify gaps, prioritize investments, and chart a deliberate path toward a composable, intelligent enterprise across critical dimensions, including architectural modularity, platform maturity, and AI integration.

Figure 2.10 Future-Readiness Assessment for Enterprise Software Delivery

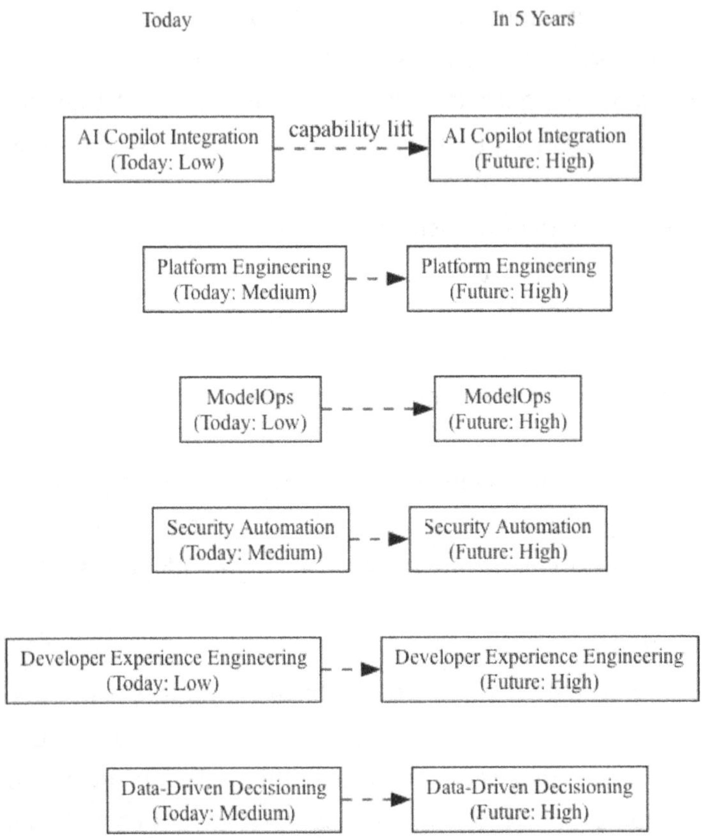

The next chapter explores how AI, particularly AI-driven engineering and autonomous pipelines, accelerates this transition and transforms the work of software teams.

Chapter 3

AI-Accelerated Engineering and Autonomous Delivery Pipelines

The rise of artificial intelligence represents the most profound shift in software engineering since the introduction of high-level programming languages. While cloud-native and composable architectures provide the structural foundation for modern enterprise systems, AI transforms the way software is built, tested, deployed, and operated. AI is no longer merely a supporting tool; its growing capabilities position it as an active participant in the engineering lifecycle.

Enterprises that master AI-accelerated engineering gain significant strategic advantages: faster delivery cycles, higher quality outputs, reduced operational burdens, lower cognitive load for engineers, and greater organizational agility. Research shows that AI-assisted development tools improve task completion time, developer satisfaction, and code quality in measurable ways [19], [21], [23], [33].

This chapter examines how AI reshapes the software development lifecycle (SDLC), the emergence of autonomous delivery pipelines, and the organizational implications of adopting AI as a co-engineer.

3.1 How AI Is Transforming the Software Development Lifecycle

AI brings step-change improvements to every phase of software delivery. Figure 3.1 highlights where AI-driven activities are added to increase speed, reliability, and quality, illustrating how intelligence is embedded end-to-end across the software lifecycle from requirements through to operations.

Figure 3.1 AI Integration Across the Software Development Lifecycle

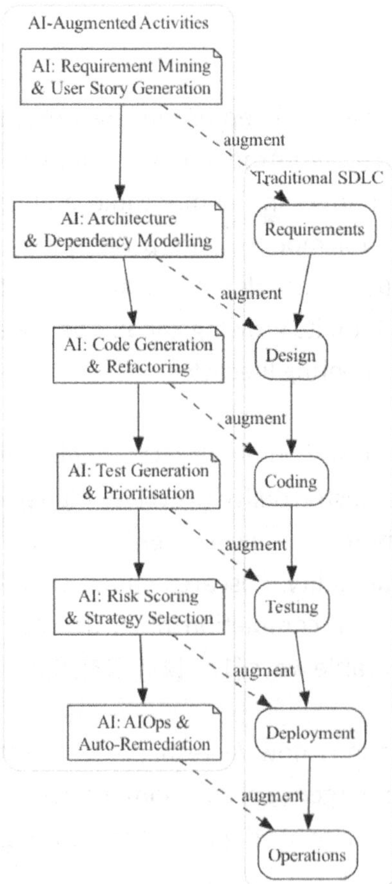

Requirements and Early Design

AI systems can analyze customer feedback, historical requirements, defect patterns, and domain-specific documents to propose requirement refinements or generate structured user stories. Early research shows that AI-assisted requirement generation can reduce ambiguity and improve alignment between business and technical stakeholders [34].

AI-assisted modelling tools can generate architecture diagrams, dependency maps, and system flowcharts from natural-language prompts or existing code repositories, providing teams with rapid visibility into complexity hotspots. Figure 3.2 illustrates an AI-driven requirements workflow that reduces ambiguity and accelerates early design by converting raw inputs into structured user stories.

Figure 3.2 AI-Driven Requirements and User Story Generation

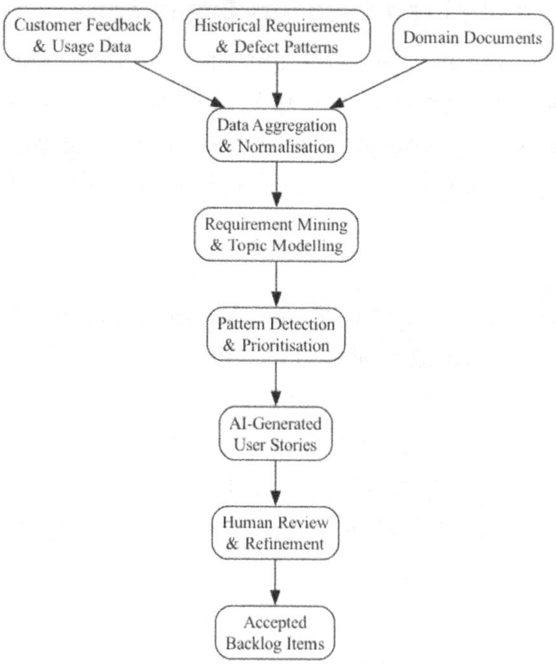

Code Generation and Enhancement

AI-powered code generation tools, particularly large language models (LLMs), have reshaped the coding process. Studies demonstrate that developers using tools such as GitHubCopilot complete tasks significantly faster, up to 55% improvement in controlled settings, while reporting increased flow state and reduced cognitive load [21], [33].

Research reveals three consistent benefits:

1. Acceleration of repetitive tasks
2. Improved consistency and adherence to standards
3. Reduction of boilerplate and low-value activities

However, these tools introduce risks: hallucinated code, subtle defects, and insecure patterns. This necessitates human oversight and governance frameworks.

AI-Augmented Testing and Quality Engineering

AI dramatically improves test creation, prioritization, and maintenance. Test-generation models can create unit, integration, and end-to-end tests from code context or behavior descriptions. Empirical studies show that AI-generated tests improve coverage and reduce manual testing effort [35].

AI-driven test selection streamlines delivery pipelines by ranking tests using signals such as historical failure trends, the predicted impact of code changes, and dependency heatmaps. This shortens cycle times while increasing confidence in release readiness. Figure 3.3 illustrates this AI-based prioritization, where multiple inputs are synthesized into a ranked execution plan that maximizes coverage and minimizes overall run time.

Figure 3.3 AI-Powered Test Prioritization Workflow

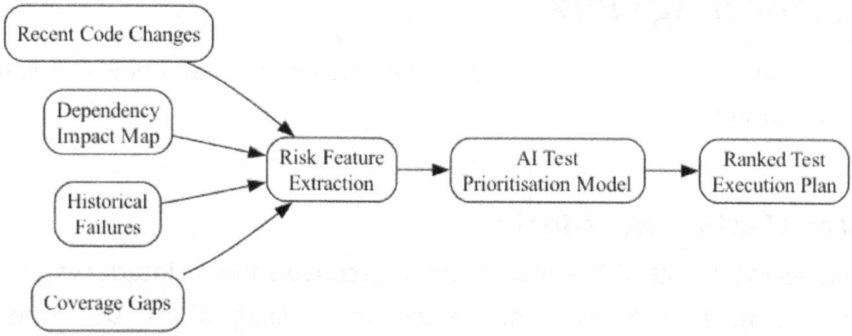

AI in Deployment, Monitoring, and Operations

AI-enabled observability systems analyze logs, metrics, and traces to detect anomalies earlier and localize root causes faster than manual methods. Research in AI-powered reliability engineering shows improved incident detection, reduced mean time to recovery (MTTR), and predictive failure analysis [36].

Machine learning techniques for anomaly detection and forecasting are increasingly embedded into modern AIOps platforms, enabling:

- Automated alert suppression
- Noise reduction
- Predictive autoscaling
- Incident clustering
- Automated remediation

These capabilities fundamentally shift operations from reactive firefighting to proactive, intelligent control.

3.2 The "Co-Engineer" Model: How AI Reshapes Engineering Work

AI is changing what it means to be a software engineer and how software is developed.

AI as a Partner, Not a Tool

Engineers interact with AI models through conversational interfaces, pair-programming workflows, and context-driven suggestions. Developers begin tasks by prompting the AI system, iterating collaboratively, and validating outputs.

This changes the engineering focus from hands-on construction to orchestration, guidance, and review. Figure 3.4 illustrates the iterative partnership between engineers and AI, showing the continuous loop of expressing intent, AI generation, human assessment, and refinement that defines modern co-engineering.

Figure 3.4 Iterative Human-AI Co-Engineering Cycle

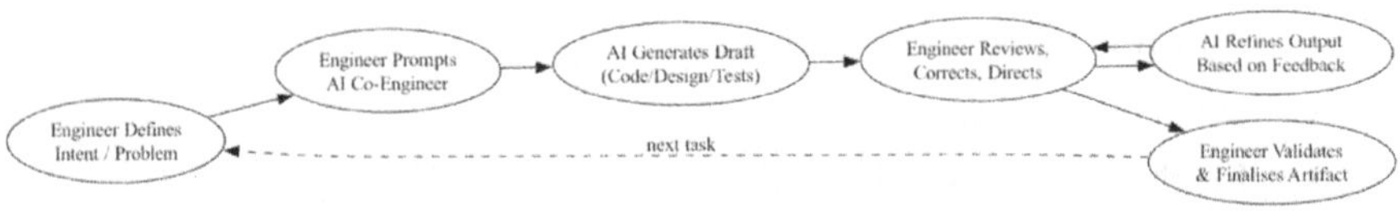

Evolving Responsibilities

As AI assumes more routine coding tasks, the human role evolves toward:

- System design
- Domain modelling
- Architectural decision-making
- Oversight and governance
- Reviewing AI outputs
- Problem decomposition

Research confirms that developers using AI spend more time on complex reasoning tasks and less time on mechanical implementation [21].

Impact on Team Structure and Skill Sets

Enterprises must rethink team structures. AI necessitates:

- new roles such as AI engineering leads, prompt engineers, and AI safety reviewers
- revised definitions of seniority
- updated expectations of engineering productivity

Teams become increasingly cross-functional, combining expertise in strategy, architecture, engineering, data, and security. Figure 3.5 presents a future team topology, introducing emerging AI-focused roles alongside traditional engineering functions to illustrate how hybrid teams are structured for effective oversight and collaboration.

Figure 3.5 Future Team Structure with AI-Centric Roles

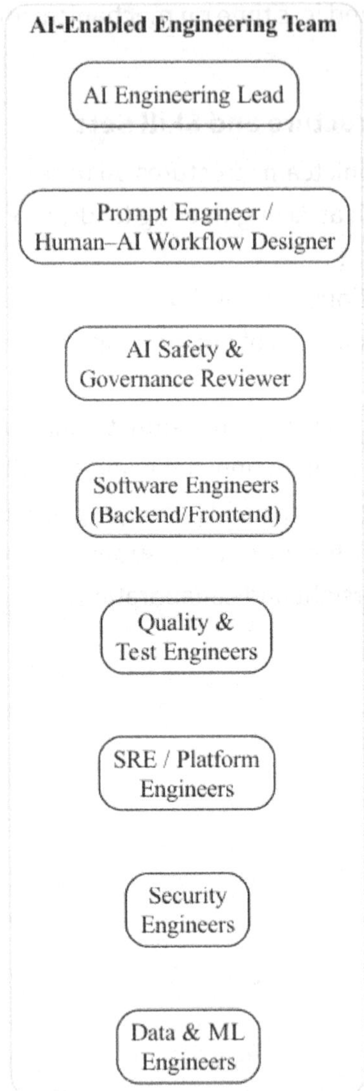

3.3 Autonomous Delivery Pipelines: From DevOps to Cognitive DevOps

Autonomous delivery pipelines represent the next evolutionary step beyond traditional DevOps automation.

From Scripted Automation to Adaptive Intelligence

Traditional CI/CD pipelines follow predefined scripts. Autonomous pipelines, in contrast, make context-aware decisions based on signals from code, architecture, security, tests, and production systems.

Examples include:

- Automated selection of relevant tests
- Dynamic determination of deployment strategy (blue-green, canary, progressive)
- Automatic rollback based on anomaly detection
- Predictive deployment risk scoring

Recent research on intelligent DevOps systems shows that AI-enhanced pipelines reduce manual intervention and significantly improve deployment speed and reliability [19].

Quality and Risk Prediction

AI can analyze commit histories, error patterns, dependency risks, and architectural complexity to predict:

- Likelihood of production defects
- Potential security vulnerabilities
- Areas with high change risk

This predictive capability supports proactive intervention instead of reactive debugging. Figure 3.6 illustrates this through a risk model that highlights key release risk indicators, including code complexity, security defects, and dependency volatility.

Figure 3.6 AI-Driven Risk Radar for Deployment Prediction

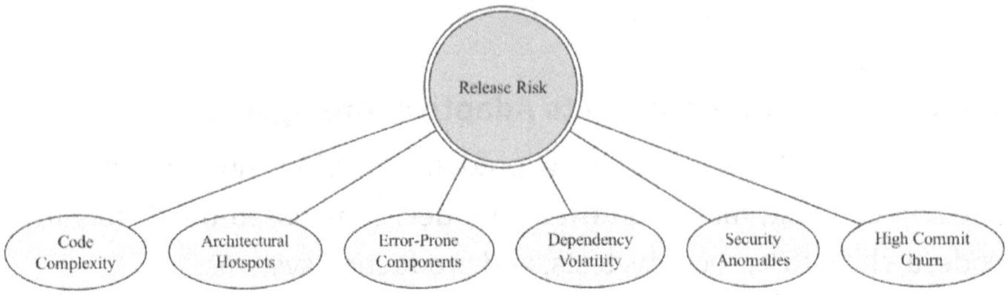

Security, Compliance, and Policy Enforcement

Policy-as-code systems combined with AI can enforce compliance automatically. AI models can detect deviations from secure coding standards, privacy requirements, or architectural patterns. This reduces the burden on security review teams and ensures continuous assurance rather than periodic audits.

3.4 The Organizational Benefits of AI-Driven Engineering

The introduction of AI across the SDLC delivers significant organizational gains.

Accelerated Delivery and Increased Throughput

AI reduces friction in coding, testing, review, and deployment. Research consistently points to increased developer velocity when AI is properly integrated [21], [33].

Higher Quality and Fewer Defects

AI identifies inconsistencies, anti-patterns, and code smells earlier. AI-enhanced static analysis tools detect vulnerabilities and risky changes before code merges.

Reduced Cognitive Load

AI handles boilerplate, routine tasks, and high-volume triage activities. Developers report improved focus, satisfaction, and mental flow [21].

Greater Predictability and Reduced Risk

Autonomous pipelines standardize delivery workflows, making release cycles more consistent and predictable. Predictive analytics helps prevent incidents, shortens recovery time (MTTR), and improves overall platform resilience. Figure 3.7 summarizes these layered benefits of AI-augmented engineering, connecting faster delivery practices to a better developer experience and, ultimately, stronger business outcomes.

Figure 3.7 Benefits of AI-Augmented Engineering

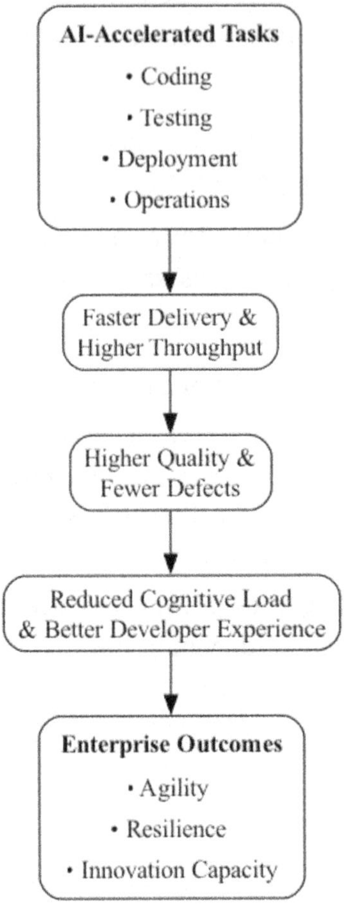

3.5 Challenges, Risks, and Governance Requirements

AI introduces new categories of risk that enterprises must manage:

Hallucinations and Inaccuracies

LLMs may produce code that is syntactically correct but semantically wrong. Research identifies hallucination as a persistent failure mode that requires human oversight [22], [37].

Security Vulnerabilities

AI-generated code may introduce insecure patterns or outdated practices. Studies highlight increases in injection risks and insecure defaults in AI-produced outputs [23].

Intellectual Property Risk

There is an ongoing debate regarding training data provenance, copyright risk, and licensing implications of AI-generated code.

Over-Reliance on AI

Developers may lose critical problem-solving skills if AI is used without proper guardrails. The co-engineer model must emphasize augmentation rather than replacement.

Bias, Inconsistency, and Drift

Models may inherit biases from training data or make inconsistent decisions across contexts. Continuous evaluation and reinforcement learning governance are required.

Enterprises must implement robust governance frameworks, including:

- Mandatory review of AI-generated artifacts
- Secure prompt engineering guidelines
- Audit trails and explainability requirements
- Controlled model updates
- Organizational AI use policies

Figure 3.8 provides a structured view of the governance challenges, grouping them into four categories: technical, security, organizational, and ethical.

Figure 3.8 AI Governance and Risk Management Framework

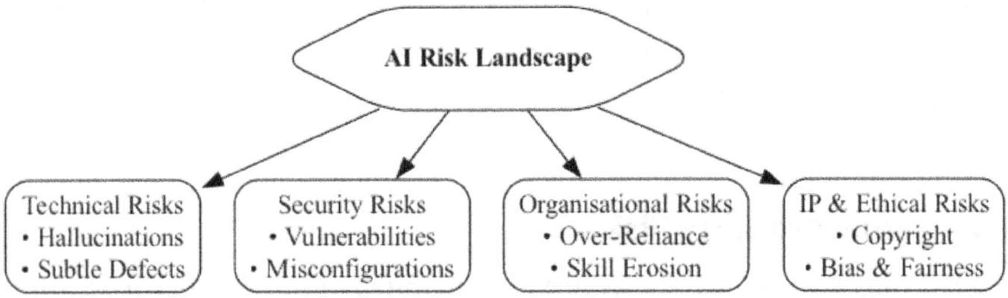

3.6 The Path Forward: Building the AI-Enabled Engineering Organization

AI-accelerated engineering and autonomous pipelines will reshape enterprise delivery over the next decade, enabling:

- Drastically faster development cycles
- Continuous experimentation and adaptation
- More resilient systems
- Higher quality and consistency
- Improved developer experience
- Lower operational burden

Figure 3.9 illustrates this future state as an integrated software delivery system in which intelligent platforms, autonomous pipelines, composable architectures, and AI co-engineers operate together. This ecosystem enables continuous testing, predictive operations, and adaptive innovation, representing the next wave of AI-enabled technology organizations.

Figure 3.9 Integrated AI-Enabled Software Delivery Ecosystem

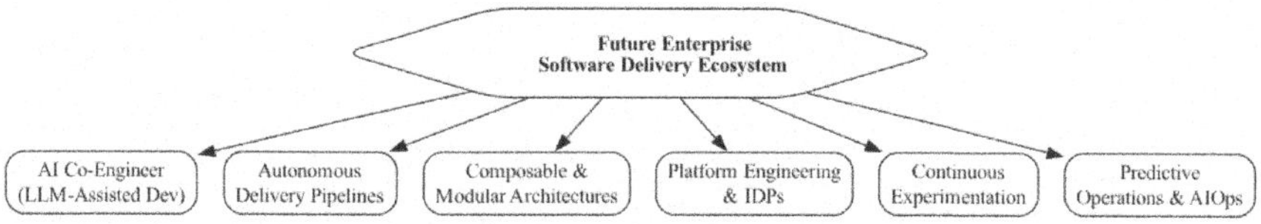

Enterprises that succeed will embrace a combination of:

1. AI-augmented engineering practices
2. Platform engineering foundations
3. Composable architectures
4. Rigorous governance and human oversight

AI does not replace human creativity, judgment, or architectural reasoning. Instead, it elevates these capabilities by removing toil and enabling engineers to focus on the work that defines competitive differentiation.

The next chapter explores how platform engineering and internal developer platforms become essential to scaling these AI-driven practices across enterprise environments.

Chapter 4

Platform Engineering and the Internal Developer Platform Revolution

Platform engineering has emerged as one of the most strategically significant developments in modern enterprise technology. As software systems scale in complexity, organizations face mounting challenges related to inconsistent tooling, duplicated effort, operational fragility, and mounting cognitive load on development teams. Research and industry analysis consistently show that these issues suppress delivery velocity, increase defect rates, and hinder enterprises' ability to innovate at the pace required by market conditions [27], [30], [38].

Internal Developer Platforms (IDPs) offer a targeted solution to these challenges. An IDP unifies tooling, workflows, environments, and standards into a cohesive, self-service platform that developers can use to build, deploy, and operate software without navigating the fragmented toolchains typical of large enterprises. Studies and industry reports indicate that organizations adopting platform engineering practices see substantial improvements in reliability, developer experience, and operational efficiency[39], [40].

Platform engineering is not simply a tooling initiative; it is a fundamental organizational shift. Much like ERP systems reshaped back-office operations in the 1990s, IDPs are reshaping how modern enterprises deliver software. This chapter explores why platform engineering has risen to prominence, how IDPs accelerate flow across the software lifecycle, and how organizations can strategically adopt this model to create high-performance engineering ecosystems.

4.1 The Problem: Tool Sprawl, Friction, and Cognitive Overload

Modern engineering organizations rely on an increasingly large ecosystem of tools: CI/CD systems, observability stacks, security scanners, Kubernetes clusters, secret managers, IaC templates, service meshes, ticketing tools, API gateways, and more. Each tool serves a purpose, but collectively they create a fragmented environment that can overwhelm developers. As PlatformEngineering.org notes, the typical developer must understand and manually integrate more than a dozen systems before deploying a single service [45].

Empirical research confirms that developers spend the majority of their time, up to 70 percent, on activities outside writing business logic, including configuration, debugging pipeline issues, or navigating complex infrastructure requirements [10]. Cognitive load, a central concept in modern platform engineering thinking, increases as developers must maintain mental models of entire distributed ecosystems [32], [41]. Higher cognitive load is associated with lower productivity, more mistakes, and longer lead times. Figure 4.1 illustrates this by showing the many tools and concepts a developer must manually connect, highlighting the fragmentation that drives excessive cognitive load and pulls attention away from business logic.

Figure 4.1 Developer Cognitive Load in Fragmented Tool Environments

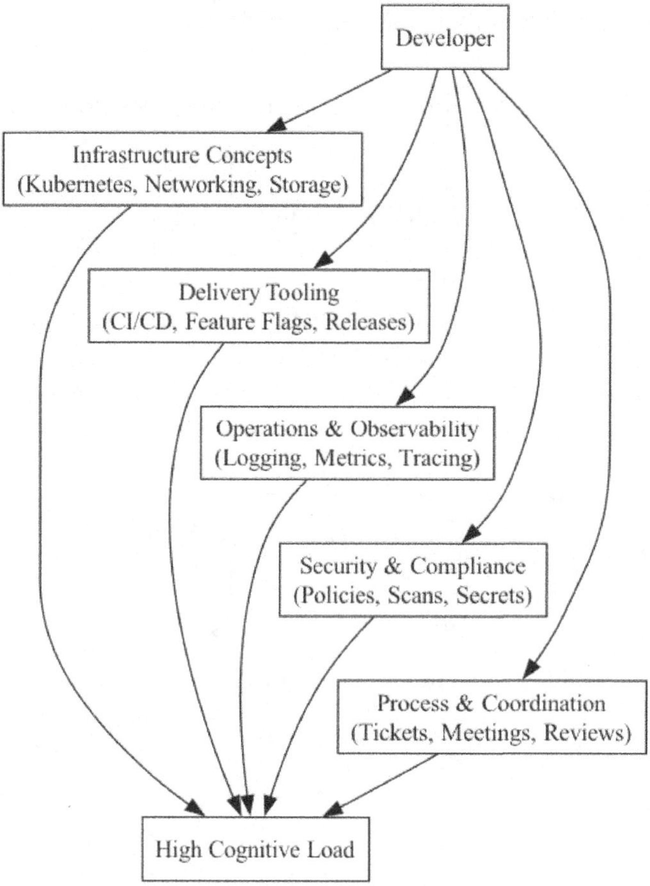

Tool sprawl leads to several strategic issues:

- Inconsistent standards across teams
- Duplicated configuration and infrastructure code
- High onboarding costs for new engineers
- Reliance on a few senior engineers to troubleshoot complexity
- Reduced delivery predictability due to variability in workflows

Without intervention, this complexity becomes self-reinforcing, creating a delivery environment that is increasingly brittle and inefficient.

Developers need to serve as manual integrators for many disconnected systems, as shown in Figure 4.2. This fragmented reality is the main cause of friction, inconsistent data, and decreased flow.

Figure 4.2 Disconnected Tool Sprawl in Enterprise Development

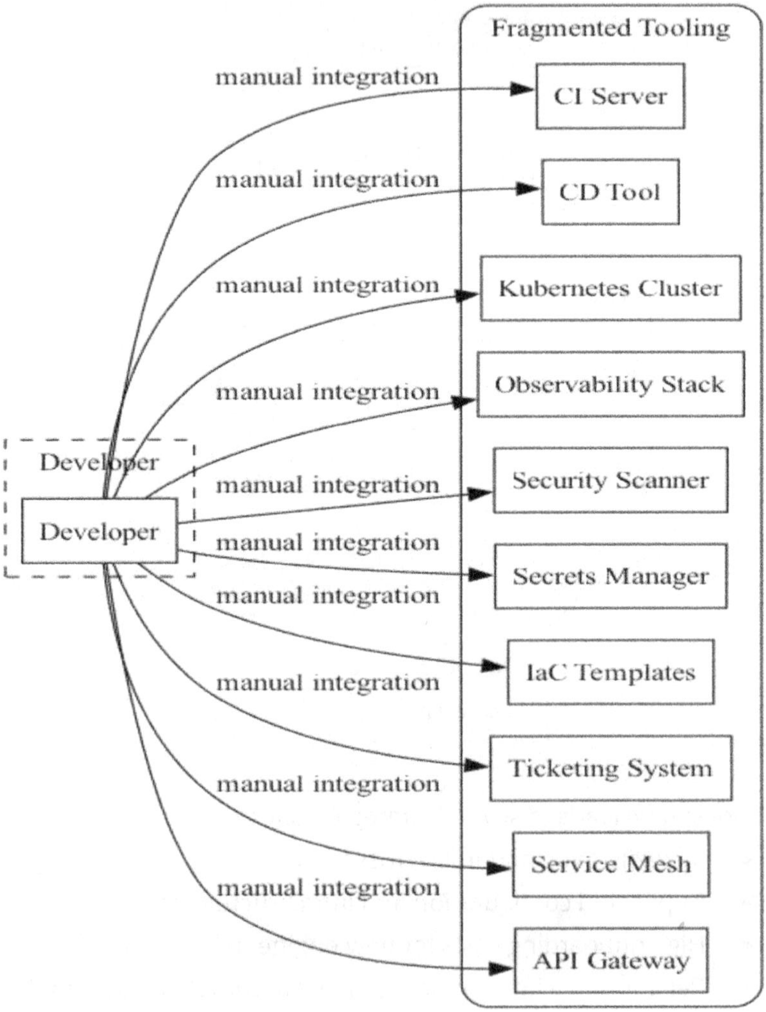

4.2 What Platform Engineering Is and Is Not

Platform engineering aims to solve these challenges by creating integrated, reusable, and automated capabilities that support the full software lifecycle. Rather than offering a loose collection of tools, platform engineering teams build internal products, platforms that provide developers with a consistent, safe, and efficient path to production [41], [42].

An Internal Developer Platform (IDP) typically includes:

- Self-service environment provisioning
- Golden-path CI/CD pipelines
- Infrastructure as code modules
- Automated security and compliance gating
- Integrated observability tooling
- Service discovery and dependency visibility
- A unified developer portal, often powered by Backstage [43], [44].

A mature IDP is structured as a layered architecture, as illustrated in Figure 4.3. The diagram shows how complexity is abstracted so product teams can operate with self-service capabilities, supported by a strong infrastructure foundation and shared services.

Figure 4.3 Layered Architecture of an Internal Developer Platform

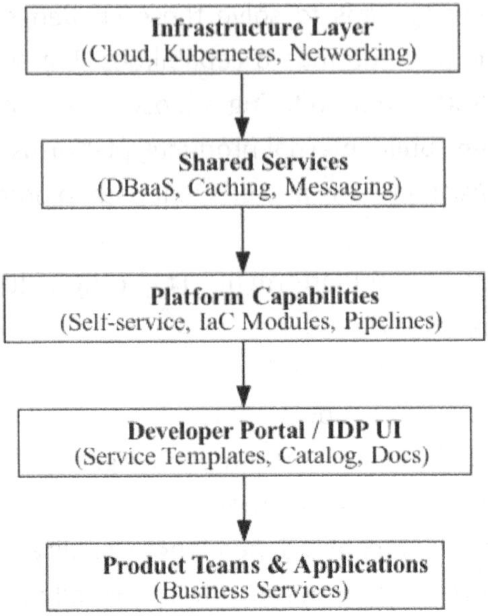

IDPs are designed to abstract complexity. Developers interact with high-level workflows that: "create service," "deploy to staging," "roll back", rather than low-level infrastructure configuration. This reduces cognitive load, eliminates unnecessary decision-making, and ensures that best practices and security standards are applied consistently [39], [42], [45].

Crucially, platform engineering is not a:

- Rebranding of DevOps
- Traditional shared services function
- Attempt to centralize control or restrict autonomy

Rather, research highlights that platform engineering operationalizes DevOps at scale, enabling autonomy by providing safe, paved paths rather than unrestricted tool sprawl [39], [42], [45].

4.3 Golden Paths: The Strategic Heart of the IDP

Golden paths are opinionated, well-supported workflows that guide teams toward optimal, compliant ways to build and deploy software. Successful IDPs emphasize the importance of offering golden paths rather than endless options, as choice overload is a major contributor to developer inefficiency [34], [46].

Golden paths encode:

- Infrastructure standards
- Security policies
- Architectural conventions
- CI/CD patterns
- Documentation and observability defaults

Figure 4.4 highlights the transformative impact of this approach, showing the shift from many bespoke decisions to a streamlined, deliberately curated "Golden Path" that lets developers concentrate on customer value and business logic.

Figure 4.4 Transition from Custom Decisions to Standardized Golden Paths

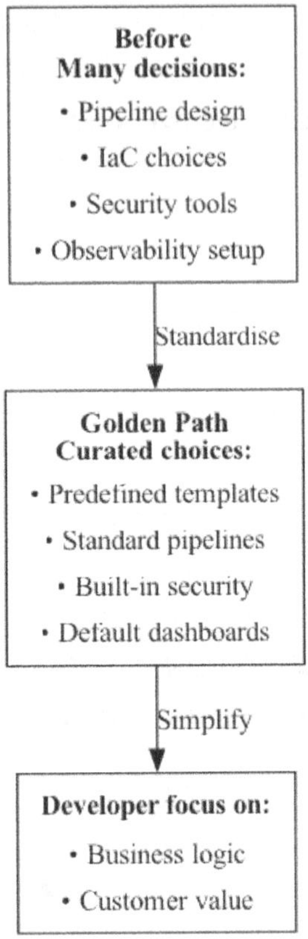

Bucchiarone et al. present reference models demonstrating how structured platform workflows reduce error rates and accelerate delivery in microservice environments [43]. Spotify's pioneering work on Backstage highlights how golden paths significantly reduce onboarding time and increase delivery consistency across large engineering organizations [44].

A golden path doesn't eliminate autonomy; it trims low-value choices so engineers can spend their time innovating instead of coordinating tooling. Figure 4.5 shows how IDP guardrails apply across the software delivery lifecycle: from design and build through deployment and operations, demonstrating how automated policies and standard patterns provide consistent safety and support.

Figure 4.5 IDP Guardrails Across the Software Delivery Lifecycle

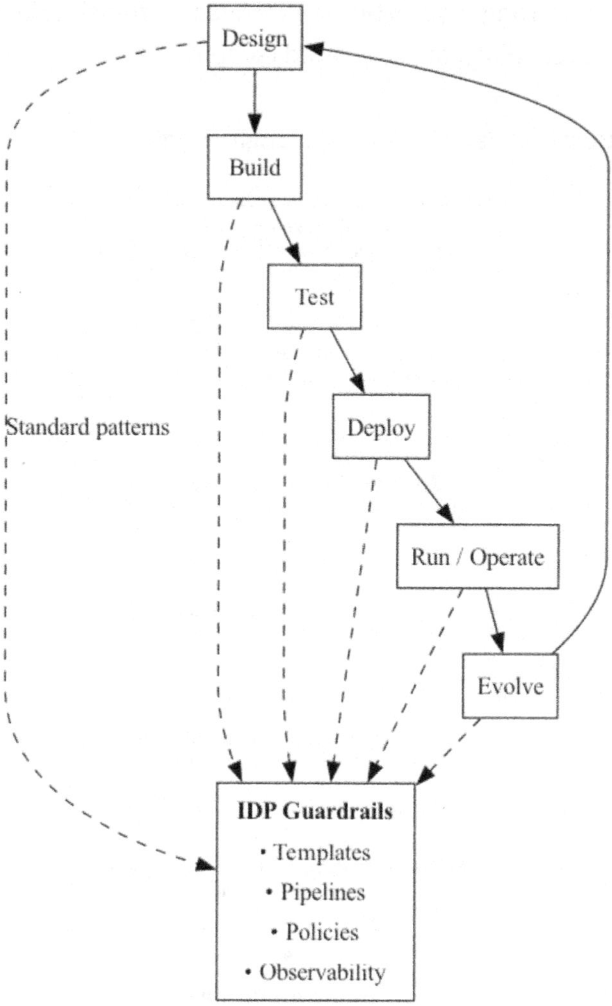

4.4 The Business Value of Platform Engineering

Platform engineering delivers both technical and strategic value, with benefits that are interconnected and mutually reinforcing. Figure 4.6 summarizes the main advantages of an IDP, showing how a better developer experience and stronger operational effectiveness translate into faster delivery, greater reliability, and improved compliance.

Figure 4.6 Business Value of Platform Engineering

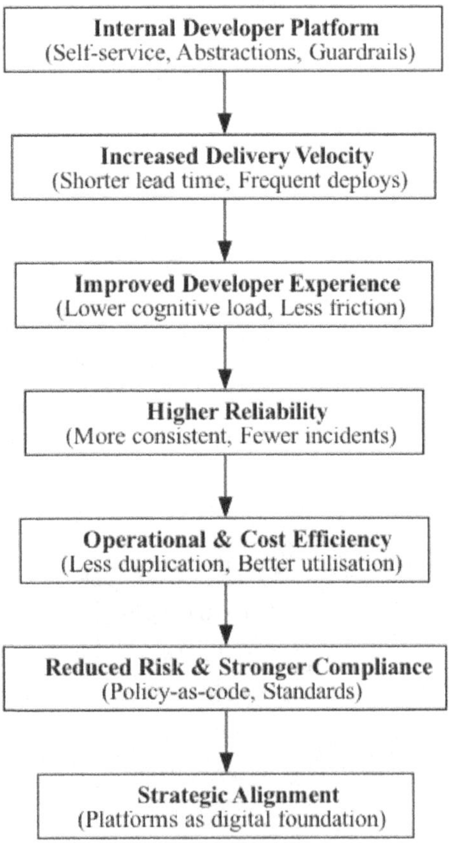

Faster Delivery Cycles

By reducing friction across development, testing, deployment, and operations, IDPs dramatically increase flow efficiency. Gartner reports that companies implementing IDPs experience notable reductions in lead time for changes and increased deployment frequency. Similarly, Port's State of IDP Report shows measurable improvements in reliability and engineering throughput across enterprises adopting internal platforms [40], [36].

Improved Developer Experience

Developer experience (DevEx) has emerged as a first-class priority for engineering organizations. Platform engineering directly supports DevEx by reducing context switching and cognitive load. Research shows strong correlations between improved DevEx, productivity, and retention [27], [32], [47].

Operational and Cost Efficiency

By consolidating tooling, enforcing standardization, and automating lifecycle tasks, IDPs reduce operational overhead and infrastructure waste. Humanitec's reference architectures highlight how centralization of environment provisioning and policy enforcement reduces long-term operational cost and risk [42], [45].

Reduced Risk and Stronger Compliance

Policy-as-code and platform-level guardrails deliver a consistent security posture across teams. Gartner emphasizes that IDPs materially improve audit readiness and reduce the likelihood of misconfigurations or security drift[39].

Strategic Technology Alignment

Platforms unify delivery processes across business units, reducing silos and aligning technology execution with enterprise business strategy. They become strategic infrastructure. An internal "digital foundation" that accelerates digital transformation.

4.5 The Operating Model of a Platform Engineering Organization

Successful platform engineering requires clear organizational boundaries and collaborative patterns.

Product Thinking

Platform teams treat developers as their customers, measuring adoption, satisfaction, and platform-driven performance outcomes. Research from PlatformEngineering.org highlights the value of dedicated platform product managers who shape roadmap priorities based on developer feedback and business objectives[46]. Figure 4.7 depicts how value connects and flows among platform engineering teams, product development teams, and business stakeholders, illustrating the continuous feedback loop that keeps the platform aligned with strategy and delivers measurable value.

Figure 4.7 Value Flow Between Platform and Product Teams

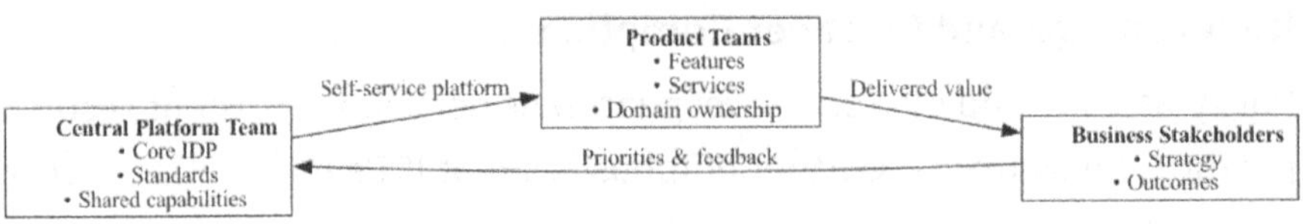

Clear Responsibilities

Platform teams own platform capabilities, while product teams own business logic. This separation of concerns reduces friction and increases delivery velocity [34].

Federated Model at Scale

Large enterprises often operate hybrid models:

- A central platform team builds core platform layers
- Domain-specific platform teams extend capabilities
- Product teams consume services via developer portals [29], [41].

This model strikes a balance between standardization and adaptability. Figure 4.8 illustrates the federated operating model, where domain-aligned platform teams extend capabilities to meet specific needs and support product teams within their domains, while a central platform team provides core standards and shared services.

Figure 4.8 Federated Platform Operating Model

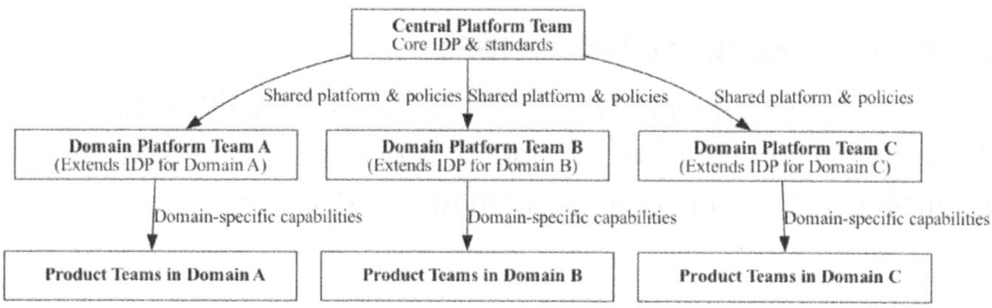

4.6 AI and the Future of Platform Engineering

AI is rapidly transforming IDPs and will define the next decade of platform engineering.

AI for Developer Guidance and Automation

AI-integrated developer portals can:

- Suggest best-fit golden paths
- Automatically generate infrastructure templates
- Detect misconfigurations, anomalies, prevent outages, and propose optimization strategies[48].
- Assist in troubleshooting deployments [43].

AI-Driven Observability and AIOps

AIOps systems embedded in the platform provide predictive analytics, automated root-cause analysis, and smart alerting, elevating operational reliability [36].

Intelligent Security and Compliance

AI can dynamically evaluate architecture decisions, dependency risks, and policy gaps during development. This transforms governance from reactive enforcement to proactive guidance.

Autonomous Pipelines Built on IDPs

AI-driven pipelines require stable abstractions. IDPs provide the predictable, mutation-controlled environments necessary for autonomous deployment strategies and governance models [42], [45].

4.7 The Strategic Future of Platform Engineering

Platform engineering is becoming a permanent, mission-critical function within modern enterprises. IDPs will evolve into intelligent, adaptive systems capable of continuous optimization and AI-assisted orchestration.

Looking ahead:

- IDPs will be foundational to enterprise transformation programs

- AI-assisted developer platforms will become standard
- Golden paths will supersede ad-hoc delivery practices
- Platform engineering teams will be central to architectural governance
- Enterprises will increasingly compete on platform maturity

Figure 4.9 shows the long-term strategic impact of platform engineering. It underscores a central point: a platform-led approach governs and flattens the complexity curve, enabling sustained growth and innovation, while ad hoc tooling creates a sharp, uncontrolled rise in complexity. Organizations that invest early in platform engineering can accelerate delivery, reduce structural complexity, and build a lasting competitive advantage in an AI-driven era.

Figure 4.9 Managing Complexity Through Platform Engineering

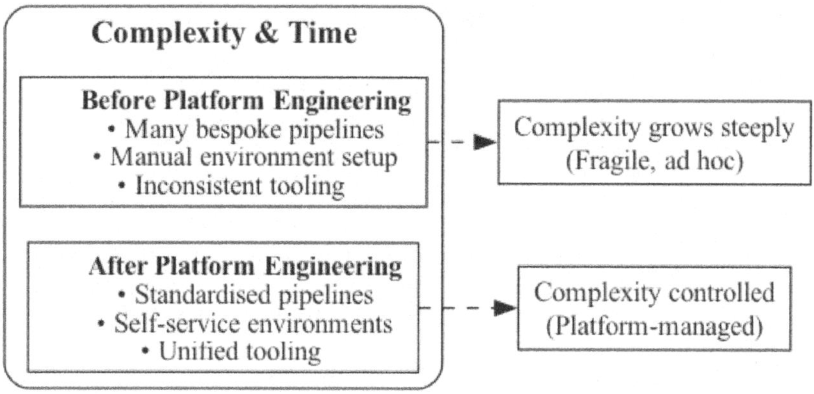

The next chapter covers security, compliance, and governance in a hyper-automated world, where cloud-native architectures and AI-enabled delivery pipelines make traditional perimeter-based controls and periodic audits ineffective. It explains how modern enterprises are shifting to Zero Trust, continuous verification, and policy-as-code to detect threats in real time and enforce compliance automatically across multi-cloud environments. It also outlines why governance must move from manual gates to embedded guardrails that scale with rapid delivery.

Chapter 5

Security, Compliance, and Governance in a Hyper-Automated World

The acceleration of software delivery, combined with cloud-native architectures and AI-enabled engineering, has introduced a fundamentally new set of security and governance challenges. Manual controls, periodic audits, and traditional perimeter-based models are no longer adequate in systems characterized by dynamic infrastructure, transient services, and autonomous pipelines. As automation becomes pervasive, security must evolve from a reactive, human-driven process into an embedded, continuous, intelligence-driven capability. Modern Zero Trust cybersecurity architectures use multiple security layers to consistently control access, verify users and systems, and enforce adaptive security policies across complex, multi-cloud enterprise environments. These frameworks leverage advanced machine-learning–based behavioural analytics to continuously monitor activity, detect threats in real time, assess risk, and identify anomalies across users, applications, and services. Alongside this, an automated compliance engine applies compliance-as-code practices to continuously assess security posture against regulatory standards and automatically enforce controls across cloud, containerized, and hybrid environments [49].

Research shows that organizations adopting automated security practices, continuous verification, zero trust, and policy-as-code experience fewer incidents, faster detection, and improved regulatory alignment[50]. This chapter examines how the threat landscape is changing, why traditional governance breaks down, and the emerging security models required to protect enterprises in a hyper-automated world.

5.1 The Changing Threat Landscape in an Automated Enterprise

The attack surface of modern systems is expanding rapidly. Cloud-native architectures distribute functionality across a constellation of services, APIs, and data pipelines. Each microservice becomes an entry point, and the complexity of these systems increases the likelihood of misconfigurations or overlooked vulnerabilities [20]. As systems become more interconnected, maintaining a security posture becomes harder without automated safeguards.

Another key shift is moving from perimeter-based to identity-centric security. Traditional firewalls and static boundaries cannot protect systems with location-agnostic, mobile, and often short-lived workloads. NIST's Zero Trust guidelines emphasize identity, continuous verification, and least privilege as the new foundations of trust [31].

The threat landscape is also accelerating. Attackers increasingly use automation and AI to scan for vulnerabilities, exploit configuration drift, and generate polymorphic attacks. Enterprises must respond at the same speed, deploying automated defenses that can identify and mitigate threats in real time.

Finally, AI systems themselves introduce unique risks. Vulnerabilities may stem from insecure AI-generated code, exposure of training data, model hallucinations, or prompt manipulation. Studies confirm that AI-generated code often contains subtle security flaws or outdated patterns that require human oversight and automated verification to detect [23], [51], [52].

5.2 The Limits of Traditional Governance Models

Traditional governance frameworks were built for slower, centrally controlled environments. Manual security reviews, ticket-driven approvals, and periodic audits cannot keep pace with organizations deploying updates multiple times per day. These manual processes create bottlenecks that slow delivery, and paradoxically, they may also decrease security: teams under pressure may bypass controls to meet deadlines or assume compliance because "the review already happened."

Governance teams also struggle to gain visibility across distributed systems. When dozens of teams deploy services independently, even understanding the current state of production becomes difficult. As a result, enterprises relying on outdated governance practices experience higher change failure rates, longer recovery times, and increased non-compliance risks [50], [53]. Figure 5.1 depicts this linear, approval-intensive process and highlights how traditional governance checkpoints create deployment delays and introduce compliance risk.

Figure 5.1 Traditional Governance Gates vs. Modern Guardrails

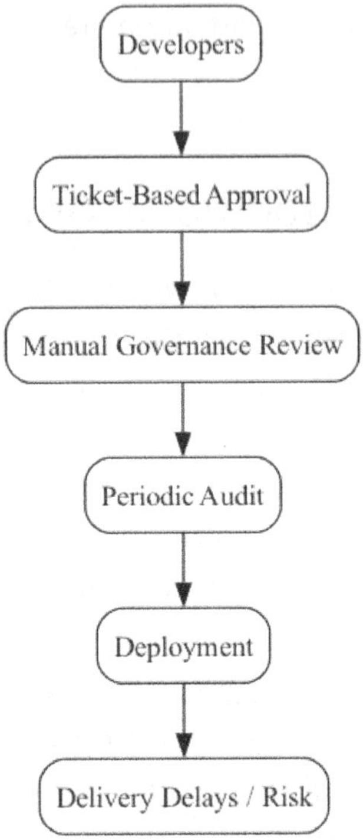

A new approach is required that shifts from gates to guardrails, from manual enforcement to automated assurance, and from periodic checks to continuous governance.

5.3 DevSecOps 2.0: Security Embedded, Automated, and Continuous

The first wave of DevSecOps introduced security scanning into CI/CD pipelines, but often in a superficial, tool-centric manner. DevSecOps 2.0 goes further by deeply embedding security into every stage of the software lifecycle.

A foundational concept is **security as code**, where security controls, policies, and compliance rules are expressed declaratively and automatically enforced. This enables consistent and scalable application of controls across teams and environments [31], [49]. Figure 5.2 demonstrates a central concept in contemporary security-as-code approaches: the transition from perimeter-focused defences to continuous identity verification, where security policies are executed continuously rather than through periodic manual checks.

Figure 5.2 Shift from Perimeter Security to Zero Trust

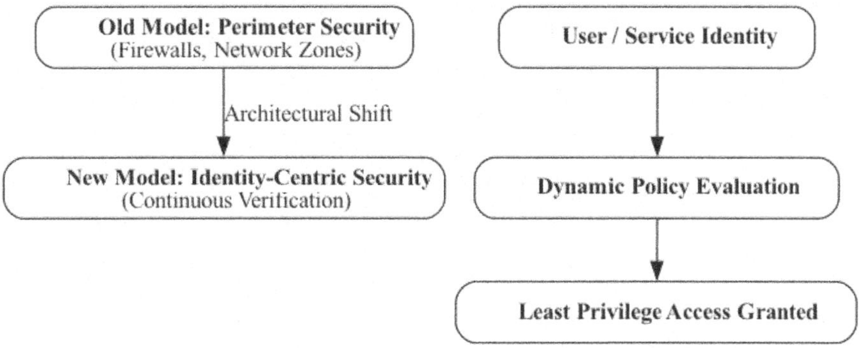

Security validation also becomes continuous. Each code change triggers automated analysis, static code analysis, dependency risk evaluation, secret scanning, infrastructure configuration checks, and container hardening reviews. Empirical evidence shows that organizations that practice continuous verification significantly reduce the likelihood that vulnerabilities reach production.

Security no longer lives exclusively at the beginning or end of development. Mature practices apply a shift-left model, encouraging early analysis, threat modelling, and secure defaults. At the same time, they embrace a shift-right mindset, employing runtime protection, anomaly detection, chaos engineering, and behavior analytics to secure systems post-deployment. Together, these models form a full-lifecycle security posture that adapts to change rather than resisting it. Figure 5.3 demonstrates an integrated security approach that incorporates both early design considerations and ongoing runtime monitoring.

Figure 5.3 Full-Lifecycle Security: Shift-Left and Shift-Right

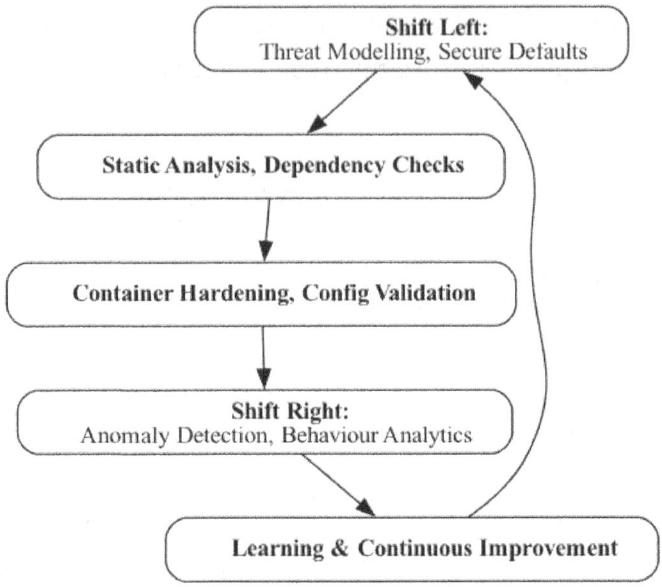

5.4 AI-Driven Security and Automated Governance

AI is increasingly central to enterprise security. In complex environments producing millions of logs and signals per minute, human analysts cannot manually correlate or interpret events. Machine learning models trained on historical behavior excel at identifying anomalies, filtering noise, and flagging high-risk events. These AIOps-driven systems improve detection speed, reduce alert fatigue, and enhance response accuracy [36].

Predictive risk scoring represents another advancement. By analyzing commit histories, dependency graphs, architectural complexity, and runtime behavior, AI can estimate the probability that a change will introduce defects or vulnerabilities [19], [51], [52]. Pipelines can use this risk score to adjust deployment strategies or require human review.

Automation also extends into remediation. AI-supported systems can revoke compromised credentials, isolate suspicious workloads, block malicious IP ranges, or roll back problematic deployments. These autonomous responses are essential in highly dynamic systems where human reaction time may be insufficient. Figure 5.4 illustrates how autonomous, AI-powered responses transform security telemetry into immediate action, enabling defence systems to operate at machine speed in situations where human reaction times are inadequate.

Figure 5.4 AI-Powered Security Detection and Automated Remediation

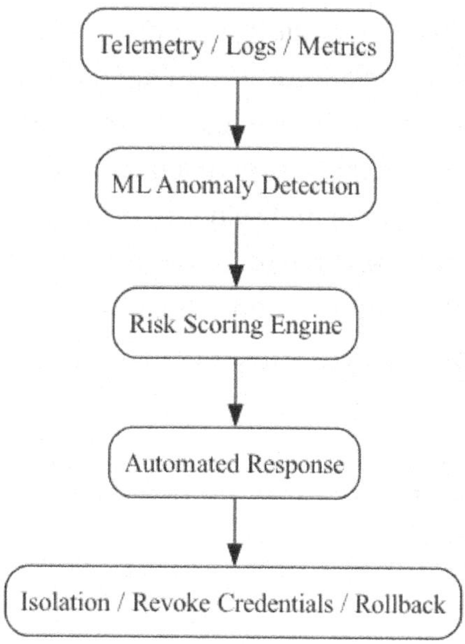

The rise of AI-generated code introduces a dual challenge: while AI boosts productivity, it also produces insecure patterns. AI-assisted static analysis tools and hybrid review workflows help mitigate these risks by automatically validating AI-generated code for correctness and compliance [22], [23].

5.5 Governance for Cloud-Native and Composable Architectures

Governance models must evolve alongside architectural changes. In modular, cloud-native environments, governance must be integrated directly into the platform layer rather than enforced through external documentation or manual checks. Internal Developer Platforms (IDPs) provide an ideal foundation for embedded governance. By offering secure templates, pre-approved architectures, and automated pathways to production, IDPs guide teams toward compliant behavior without sacrificing autonomy [29], [42], [45].

Compliance processes themselves must also adapt. Rather than generating evidence retrospectively, organizations increasingly rely on automated evidence collection, audit logs, configuration snapshots, identity activity trails, and pipeline approvals that are continuously recorded and centrally accessible. This shift enables real-time compliance monitoring and dramatically reduces the cost of regulatory audits[42], [45], [46]. Figure 5.5 illustrates how automated evidence collection transforms compliance into a continuous, real-time process rather than a retrospective exercise. By automatically capturing and validating audit trails, configuration snapshots, and approval logs, regulatory audits become significantly less time-consuming and costly.

Figure 5.5 Continuous Compliance Through Automated Evidence Collection

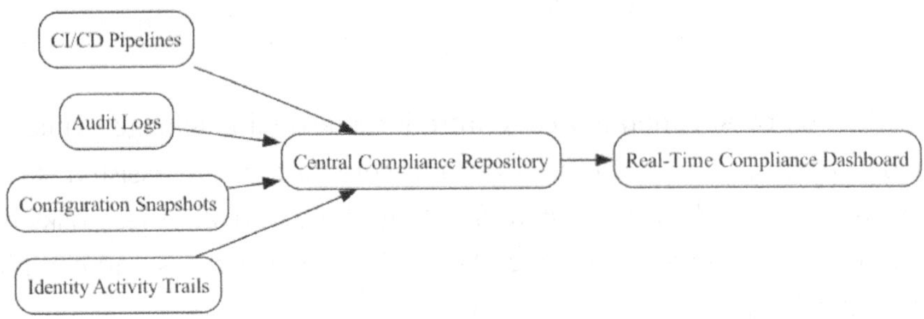

Modern governance embraces a federated model. Teams retain autonomy over their services but operate within guardrails defined by the platform and security organizations. These guardrails include baseline security controls, dependency policies, architectural standards, and data governance requirements. Research shows that this federated approach balances consistency with flexibility more effectively than either fully centralized or decentralized models [30], [55]. Figure 5.6 illustrates this federated structure, showing how domain-specific platforms, product teams, and centralized policy mechanisms operate together to enable governance at scale without compromising team velocity.

Figure 5.6 Federated Governance Model for Modern Enterprises

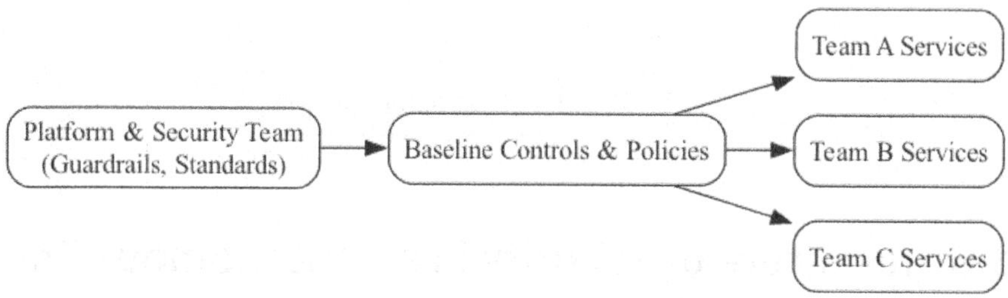

Zero Trust principles underpin this new governance model. Figure 5.7 summarizes the core principles of Zero Trust Architecture, as defined in frameworks such as NIST. It illustrates how traditional perimeter-based trust assumptions are replaced by continuous verification of identity, device posture, and contextual signals. Instead of assuming trust based on network location or historical access, systems continuously verify identities, policies, and behaviors. NIST's Zero Trust Architecture framework formalizes these principles and provides a guiding reference for enterprise adoption [31].

Figure 5.7 Zero Trust Architecture Principles

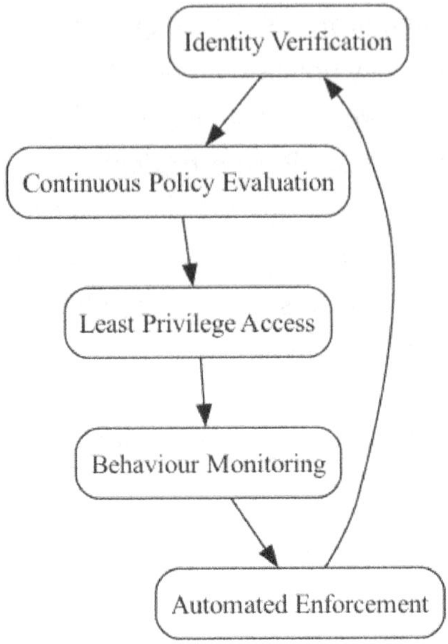

5.6 The Future of Security in an Autonomous Enterprise

Security in the autonomous enterprise will be more integrated, intelligent, and adaptive than ever before. Pipelines will enforce compliance automatically; runtime systems will detect and respond to threats before humans intervene; and governance will shift from manual oversight to machine-enforced policy.

Future-state characteristics include:

- Automated deployment gates informed by AI-driven risk scores
- Platforms that self-heal and self-secure through autonomous remediation
- Continuous behavioral analysis to detect novel attack patterns
- Governance frameworks integrated into developer tooling and environments

- Security training enhanced by AI simulations and scenario modelling

In this model, compliance becomes a by-product of engineering rather than a separate activity. Security becomes a continuous lifecycle function rather than an isolated review stage. And governance evolves into a dynamic system of adaptive controls rather than rigid, point-in-time mandates.

Enterprises that modernize their security posture will unlock faster delivery, stronger resilience, and greater organizational confidence in deploying change. Those that do not will face growing operational risk, regulatory exposure, and competitive disadvantage.

In the next chapter, we examine how AI-enabled development environments, specifically using Cursor, fundamentally change the engineering workflow and enable disciplined teams to achieve order-of-magnitude gains in development productivity.

Chapter 6

Strategies to Achieve 10× Development Productivity with Cursor

Software engineering productivity has historically advanced through new languages, automation, frameworks, and development methodologies. Yet none of these shifts have delivered the magnitude of acceleration now made possible by AI-enabled development environments. Cursor and its competitors represent a new class of AI-driven engineering tools that combine repository-wide understanding, multi-file reasoning, conversational prompting, and continuous context awareness. These capabilities allow software teams to achieve dramatic increases in development velocity while maintaining or improving quality.

Research on AI-assisted development environments consistently shows significant productivity gains. GenAI tools have a significant positive impact on software development, and organizational support is crucial to maximizing their benefits. Using Code Generation Assistants such as GitHub Copilot, ChatGPT, and Gemini in software development environments increases productivity, improves code quality, and accelerates professional learning. Additionally, they facilitate the automation of repetitive tasks, allowing focus on more complex challenges[56]. Additional studies confirm that AI-assisted coding shifts engineering effort away from boilerplate tasks and toward design, architectural decision-making, and higher-order reasoning. When systematically integrated into enterprise workflows, AI-accelerated environments create the conditions for an order-of-magnitude increase in productivity [57].

This chapter outlines strategies for safely achieving 10× development productivity using Cursor, emphasizing accuracy, guardrails, and disciplined enterprise adoption.

6.1 Why Cursor was chosen

Cursor was chosen as the primary reference in this book because, at the time of writing, it represented the most mature AI-enabled development environment with strong repository-wide reasoning, multi-file context, and features explicitly suited to enterprise-scale software delivery. While Cursor serves as a concrete and practical exemplar throughout the chapter, the principles, strategies, and governance models described are tool-agnostic and will apply equally to new and more advanced AI development platforms as they inevitably emerge. The reference to Cursor does not constitute a recommendation, and the principles discussed are intentionally tool-agnostic and applicable across current and future platforms.

6.2 Why AI-Enhanced Development Environments Are Transformational

Traditional IDEs provide static assistance: syntax highlighting, autocomplete, and debugging tools, but they do not meaningfully participate in the composition or comprehension of software. Cursor fundamentally changes this dynamic. It is an active collaborator capable of generating code across multiple files, understanding project intent, mapping dependencies, and providing instant reasoning about unfamiliar portions of the codebase.

Several factors drive its transformational impact. AI tools dramatically reduce the time spent on repetitive tasks, boilerplate creation, and low-level implementation details. Experimental studies show that developers using AI pair-programming tools not only complete tasks faster but also enter a peak performance psychological state known as "flow", more frequently, improve code comprehension, and accelerate onboarding to unfamiliar systems .

AI also enhances large-scale code comprehension. Cursor can summarize codebases, explain architectural intent, and generate dependency maps. These activities typically consume significant time, particularly in legacy or complex environments. Research highlights that repository-level understanding reduces onboarding time for new engineers and accelerates modification work [58].

AI further accelerates refactoring and structural changes. Recent evaluations of LLM-based refactoring tools show strong performance in applying large, multi-file refactoring, especially when guided through iterative, step-by-step prompting [59]. These capabilities are invaluable in enterprises where technical debt, legacy systems, and architectural drift suppress innovation.

AI-assisted environments also reduce cognitive load by providing an always-available reasoning partner. Developers no longer need to mentally track all dependencies or manually traverse large modules. The AI becomes a persistent augmentation of memory and context. This reduction in cognitive burden is strongly correlated with enhanced developer productivity and satisfaction.

Together, these effects fundamentally reshape the engineering workflow and create unprecedented opportunities for exponential productivity improvements.

6.3 Foundational Principles for Effective Cursor Use

Achieving 10× productivity is not the result of sporadic AI use but rather of disciplined, structured workflows. Effective adoption requires a shift from viewing Cursor as a suggestion engine to treating it as a co-engineer with specific responsibilities and constraints.

A key principle is working iteratively in small increments rather than issuing monolithic prompts. Research on prompt engineering and reasoning tasks demonstrates that decomposition significantly improves the accuracy, reasoning depth, and reliability of LLM outputs [54], [55]. Smaller tasks yield more predictable, verifiable results.

Anchoring AI in real code is similarly essential. By referencing explicit files, functions, and architectural patterns, developers reduce hallucination risk and increase alignment between generated output and project conventions.

Frequent validation is another foundational practice. Rather than accepting AI-generated code at face value, engineers should create a rapid cycle of generation, inspection, refinement, and testing. This aligns with findings that AI generates useful "first drafts" but requires systematic review to ensure correctness and compatibility[57]. Figure 6.1, which depicts the continuous process of generation, verification, refinement, and evaluation that defines a successful AI-human partnership, captures the crucial cooperation between AI buildup and human control.

Figure 6.1 Iterative AI-Human Collaboration Workflow

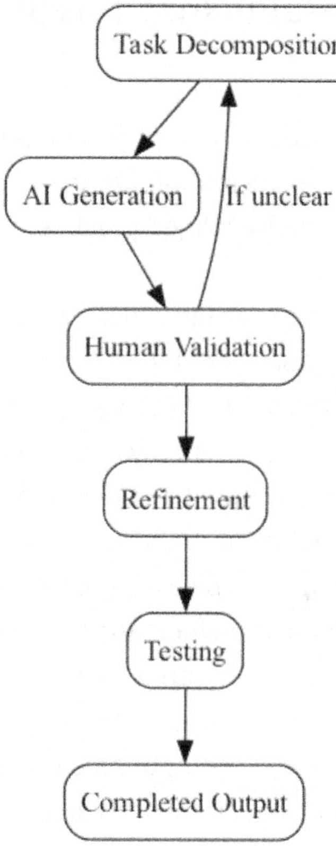

Leveraging Cursor's multi-file reasoning is another critical success factor. The ability to implement cross-cutting changes, propagate renames, or restructure domain boundaries in a single coordinated operation dramatically reduces engineering effort. Research shows that multi-file LLM reasoning substantially outperforms single-prompt generation in terms of consistency and correctness.

Finally, teams must maintain architectural intent. AI will follow the patterns it sees; if the codebase contains technical debt, inconsistencies, or outdated design, Cursor may reinforce or amplify them. Clean architectures, consistent naming, and documented patterns increase both accuracy and long-term maintainability.

6.4 Eliminating Hallucinations and Ensuring Accuracy

Hallucinations represent the primary risk associated with LLM-assisted development. However, hallucination frequency and severity can be significantly reduced through disciplined practices.

Decomposing work into smaller, well-defined components consistently reduces hallucination risk. By separating features into discrete prompts for data structures, business logic, input validation, and error handling, developers can incrementally review and validate each element with greater accuracy and control [52]. Constraining prompts is equally effective. By specifying exact inputs, expected outputs, target files, or architectural patterns, developers reduce ambiguity and limit the degrees of freedom that often produce hallucinations. Studies show that explicit prompt constraints improve correctness across a wide range of code-generation tasks. Figure 6.2 depicts this systematic approach to ensuring accuracy by presenting the core components of a hallucination-reduction model based on task decomposition and external validation.

Figure 6.2 Hallucination-Reduction Framework through Decomposition and Verification

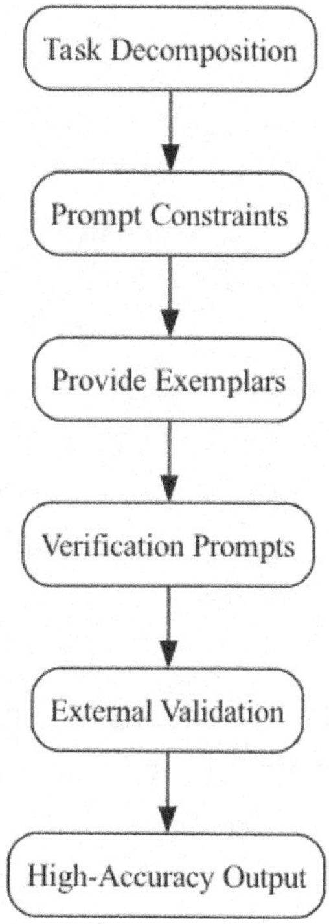

Providing exemplars and verified patterns from existing codebases further reduces risk. LLMs are pattern-driven systems; anchored examples significantly increase both structural and semantic fidelity.

Figure 6.3 illustrates the relationship between architectural patterns, explicit constraints, and aligned AI output, demonstrating how constrained prompting steers AI generation toward greater accuracy and consistency.

Figure 6.3 Architectural Pattern-Aligned Prompting with Constraints

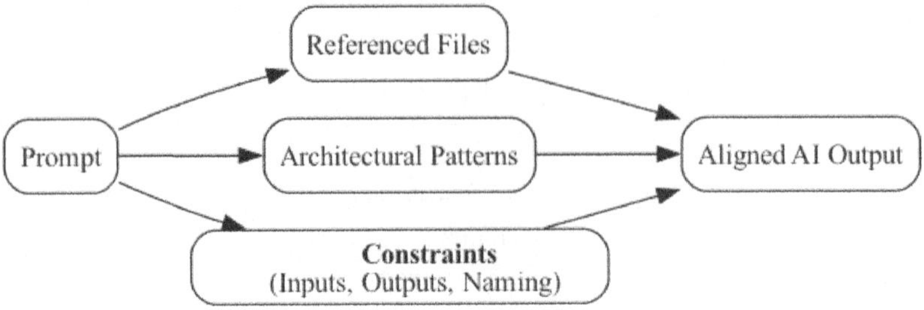

Verification prompts add an additional safeguard. Developers can instruct Cursor to identify potential bugs, list assumptions, explain design choices, or generate test cases. Research on AI-powered software testing confirms that these verification prompts detect defects that would otherwise escape initial review [2], [56].

Finally, external validation remains indispensable. Static analysis, security scanning, and automated test execution consistently reveal issues in AI-generated code LLMs accelerate code creation; automated tools ensure that acceleration does not compromise quality.

6.5 Productivity Workflows for Achieving 10× Output

Cursor supports several high-leverage workflows that enable exponential productivity gains.

Rapid prototyping is one. Engineers can move from concept to workable implementation in minutes by asking Cursor to scaffold new modules, define APIs, or generate UI components. This dramatically reduces time spent on initial implementation or proof-of-concept development.

Multi-step refactoring workflows represent another powerful capability. Recent studies on LLM-driven refactoring show that AI can safely execute cross-cutting transformations when guided through staged prompts and verification cycles [58], [59]. Figure 6.4 presents this structured refactoring approach, illustrating how AI-assisted refactoring progresses through pattern alignment, coordinated cross-file changes, localized updates, and continuous verification of structural integrity.

Figure 6.4 Staged AI-Accelerated Refactoring Pipeline

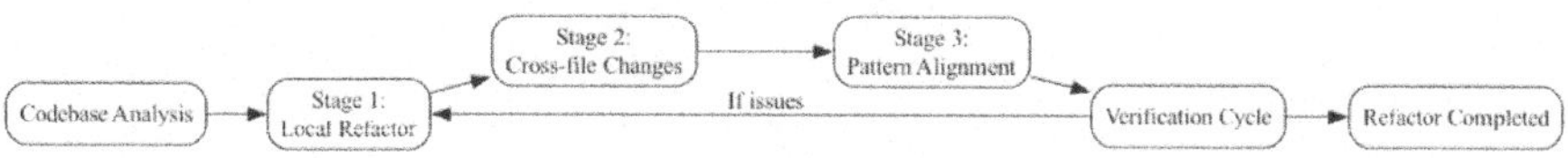

Enterprises with large codebases often spend months on refactoring projects; Cursor can significantly compress these cycles.

Documentation becomes a natural byproduct of engineering. Cursor can generate internal documentation, function explanations, and architectural summaries. This improves maintainability and reduces the overhead typically associated with documentation tasks.

Testing workflows are also massively accelerated. AI-generated tests increase coverage, identify edge cases, and highlight assumptions in the code. Entire test suites can be produced in minutes, especially when combined with repository-wide visibility.

Figure 6.5 depicts the complete AI-driven testing workflow, demonstrating how AI-generated tests support automated execution, uncover edge cases, and provide feedback that enhances implementation quality.

Figure 6.5 AI-Driven Testing and Quality Enhancement Loop

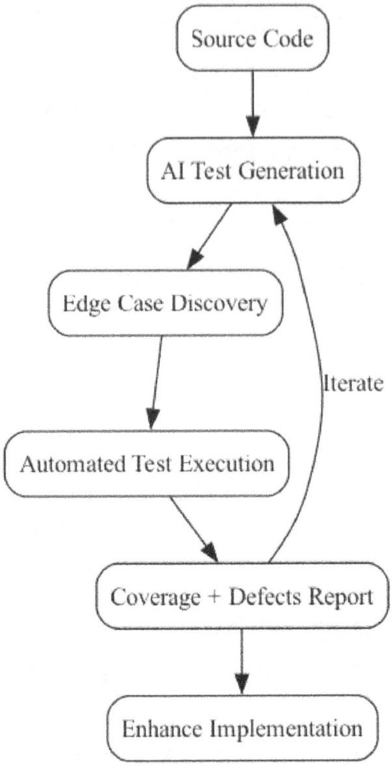

Debugging is similarly enhanced. Cursor can analyze stack traces, reason about failure modes, and propose remediation strategies. This reduces the time required to diagnose complex issues across distributed systems.

Cursor also promotes architectural consistency. Developers can instruct the AI to apply specific patterns or enforce consistent naming conventions across files. This reduces architectural drift and ensures greater long-term coherence in the codebase.

6.6 Integrating Cursor into Enterprise Delivery Environments

Cursor becomes most effective when integrated deeply into enterprise delivery ecosystems.

Coupling Cursor with Internal Developer Platforms ensures that AI-generated code adheres to platform standards and runtime expectations. Golden paths, secure templates, and policy-as-code frameworks guide AI output toward compliant implementations. Figure 6.6 shows the integrated enterprise delivery model, illustrating how developer platforms, AI tooling, governance frameworks, architectural documentation, and CI/CD pipelines combine to enable enterprise-grade software delivery.

Figure 6.6 Enterprise AI-Integrated Software Delivery Model

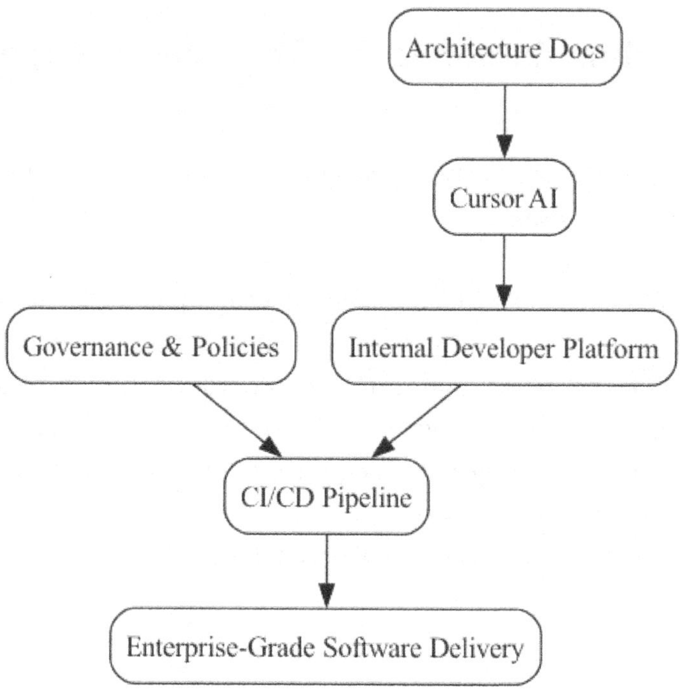

Alignment with CI/CD pipelines is essential. AI-generated code should undergo the same testing, scanning, and approval processes as human-generated code. This ensures that acceleration does not introduce operational or security risks.

Enterprises should also embed architectural decision records, domain models, and style guides into Cursor's contextual prompts. When given access to architectural documentation, Cursor produces outputs that better align with system intent.

A robust governance framework must also clarify the boundaries of AI usage. What types of work AI may perform, what requires human oversight, and what approval flows govern large-scale automated changes. Governance disciplines ensure both safety and consistency across teams.

6.7 Scaling Cursor Across Engineering Organizations

Achieving 10× productivity requires organization-wide adoption, not isolated individual usage.

Enterprises should create standard usage patterns and repeatable workflows for core engineering tasks: feature creation, debugging, refactoring, documentation, and testing. Standardization reduces ambiguity and accelerates learning. Figure 6.7 illustrates the progression toward organizational AI maturity, beginning with standardized workflows and advancing through team training, evaluation, and knowledge sharing to achieve fully AI-enabled engineering capability.

Figure 6.7 Organizational AI Engineering Maturity Framework

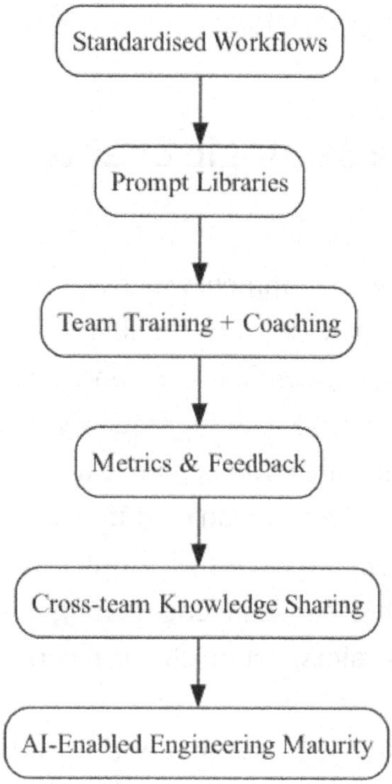

Prompt libraries accelerate adoption and reduce hallucinations. Shared prompt templates for common actions: creating services, implementing controllers, generating tests, writing SQL, making AI assistance repeatable and predictable.

Training and coaching are essential. Engineering teams must learn to decompose prompts, use structured iteration, and employ verification strategies. AI changes the engineer's skill profile from implementer to orchestrator.

Measurement provides feedback loops. Organizations should track delivery metrics, code quality, defect rates, and developer satisfaction to refine their AI-enabled workflows.

Finally, cross-team knowledge sharing builds maturity. AI techniques evolve quickly; communities of practice ensure that the best patterns propagate across the enterprise.

6.8 Cursor as a Strategic Enabler of the Future Enterprise

AI-driven engineering environments such as Cursor represent a structural breakthrough in software delivery capability. When combined with platform engineering, modern architecture, and automated governance, Cursor allows enterprises to deliver high-quality software faster, with fewer errors, and at dramatically lower cognitive and operational cost.

Cursor does not replace human engineers; it elevates them. Engineers become strategic problem-solvers who direct, validate, and refine AI-generated output. The highest-value engineering work is defining intent, architecture, and constraints, not mechanical coding.

Enterprises that adopt Cursor thoughtfully will gain capabilities far beyond speed. They will reduce technical debt, improve quality, strengthen governance, accelerate onboarding, and unleash a level of engineering creativity that was previously constrained by manual effort.

In the next chapter, we explore how these shifts transform team structures, operating models, and the nature of engineering work itself.

In the next chapter, we examine how AI-accelerated development reshapes the structure of engineering teams, the skills required of modern engineers, and the operating models that govern enterprise delivery. As AI becomes a permanent collaborator in software creation, organizations must evolve their talent strategies, team design, and ways of working to sustain continuous innovation at scale.

Chapter 7

The Future Operating Model: Talent, Teams, and Continuous Innovation

The rapid evolution of enterprise software delivery, driven by cloud-native architectures, platform engineering, and AI-accelerated development, is forcing organizations to rethink their operating models. Traditional structures centered on functional silos, manual governance, rigid planning cycles, and heavyweight processes cannot support the speed, autonomy, and adaptability required in modern engineering environments. Research in continuous software engineering shows that enterprises must adopt operating models optimized for fast flow, rapid learning, and continuous innovation [5], [12], [17].

At the same time, AI is reshaping the nature of engineering work itself. The rise of AI pair-programming tools, automated reasoning systems, and intelligent platforms requires new skills, new roles, and new forms of human–AI collaboration. Studies on the future of work and human–AI hybrid teams emphasize that organizations must deliberately redesign team structures, responsibilities, and workflows to fully realize the benefits of these technologies [60], [61].

This chapter outlines how talent, team structures, and operating models must evolve to support the next decade of enterprise software delivery.

7.1 How AI Reshapes Enterprise IT Roles and Talent Models

AI fundamentally shifts how software is built and the types of skills required to build it.

Engineers increasingly act as orchestrators, evaluators, and conceptual designers, directing AI systems rather than manually implementing every detail. Studies show that AI-assisted developers spend more time on reasoning, system design, and domain modelling, while spending less time on repetitive coding tasks.

The Evolution of the Engineer's Role

The modern engineer must become proficient in:

- Defining intent and constraints
- Translating problems into structured prompts
- Validating AI output for correctness and alignment
- Understanding system-wide impacts of generated code

This new skill set fundamentally reshapes the engineer's day-to-day work. Figure 7.1 illustrates this shift, showing how strategic, human-led activities are combined with the delegation of mechanical execution to AI systems.

Figure 7.1 Task Delegation Between Human and AI in Engineering

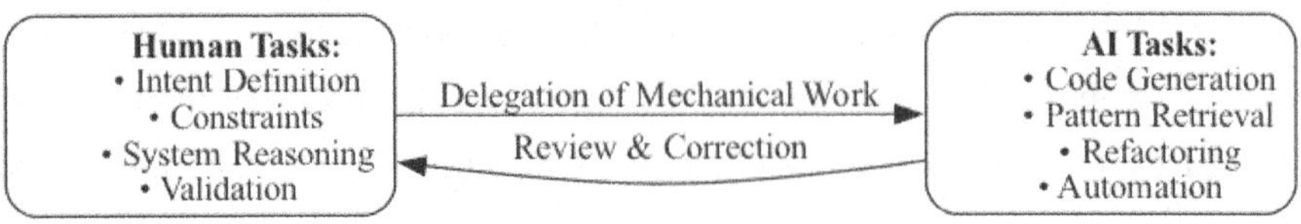

AI handles mechanical tasks, while humans focus on conceptual clarity, trade-offs, risk evaluation, and long-term maintainability. Research on future digital work structures supports this redistribution of cognitive labor, emphasizing roles in which human judgment and strategic reasoning remain essential [62].

Emerging AI-Centric Roles

Several new roles are becoming prominent in high-performing, AI-enabled organizations:

Role	Responsibility
AI Engineering Leads	AI usage patterns, prompting standards, and best practices
Prompt Engineers	Designing reusable prompt libraries and workflows
AI Governance Specialists	Ensure compliance, safety, and responsible AI adoption
Machine Teaching Specialists	Curating examples and rules to improve model behavior

These roles parallel the emergence of SRE roles in the DevOps era and reflect findings that hybrid teams require new forms of expertise to coordinate AI systems effectively.

These roles are defined by clear responsibilities rather than vague titles. Figure 7.2 outlines how they interact to establish standards, ensure security, and maximize the value of AI augmentation across the organization.

Figure 7.2 Emerging Roles for Governing and Scaling AI-Augmented Engineering

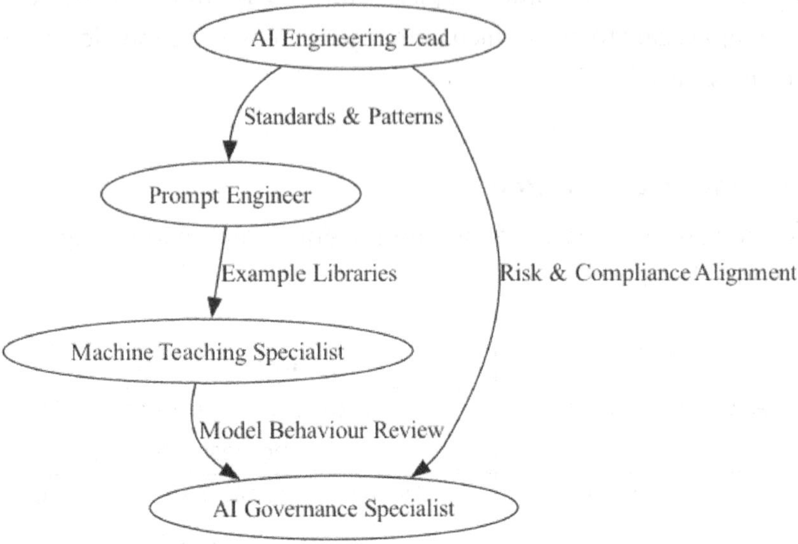

Domain Expertise as a Core Differentiator

As AI reduces implementation costs, competitive advantage shifts toward domain mastery, customer understanding, and problem framing. High-performing teams consistently demonstrate deep knowledge of the domains they serve, enabling them to make better decisions and leverage AI more effectively [2], [11].

7.2 Future Skills for High-Performance Hybrid Teams

AI-enabled development environments do not reduce the need for skills; they change which skills matter most. High-performing hybrid teams combine human creativity, reasoning, and domain insight with AI's speed, pattern recognition, and scalability.

Problem Decomposition and Prompt Structuring

Decomposition is a critical skill. Research shows that breaking problems into smaller subcomponents significantly improves LLM accuracy and reduces hallucinations[51], [52]. Rather than relying on a single prompt, this capability enables a structured, iterative workflow. Figure 7.3 illustrates this essential cycle, moving from human-led decomposition and prompting through AI generation and back to human validation.

Figure 7.3 Structured Workflow for AI-Human Code Collaboration

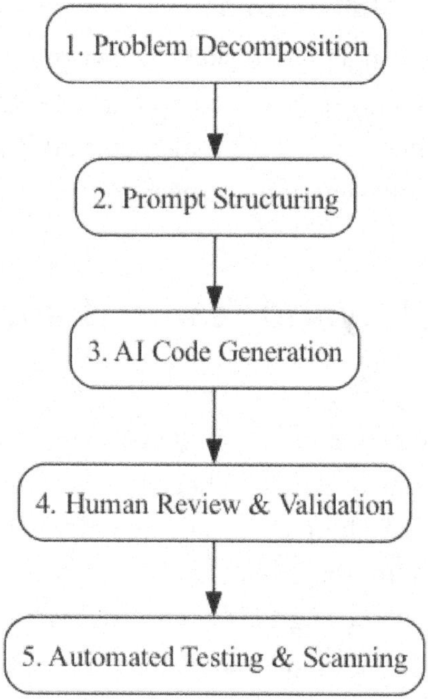

Architectural and Systems Thinking

AI can generate code, but it does not inherently understand scalability, clean architecture, performance, or long-term evolution. Engineers must therefore guide AI within architectural constraints and ensure coherence across modules. This aligns with continuous software engineering principles that emphasize emergent design and sustainable architectures[52].

Verification, Testing, and Governance

Human oversight remains crucial. Studies on AI-generated code show a non-trivial risk of subtle bugs, insecure patterns, or inconsistencies[57]. Engineers must validate AI outputs through:

- Careful review
- Targeted testing
- Architectural conformance checks
- Automated pipelines and scanners

Cross-Functional Collaboration

Modern teams increasingly blend skills across engineering, product, design, data, and compliance. Research on team design for fast flow highlights how cross-functional, domain-aligned teams accelerate decision-making and reduce coordination overhead [55], [63].

7.3 The Rise of Hybrid Teams: Humans + AI Working Together

The defining characteristic of future delivery organizations is the emergence of hybrid human–AI teams. These teams leverage AI as a partner, not a replacement, with humans providing judgment, context, and strategy. The hybrid team model is built on a clear partnership that brings together complementary strengths. Figure 7.4 summarizes the core cognitive division, highlighting where human judgment excels and where AI capabilities provide the greatest advantage.

Figure 7.4 Complementary Strengths in Human-AI Collaboration

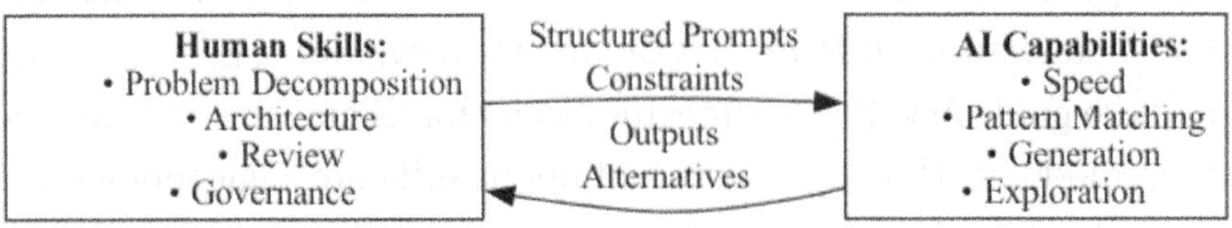

Reallocation of Cognitive Labor

This division of strengths becomes clear when comparing the areas where AI provides the greatest leverage with those where human judgment remains essential.

Humans excel at	AI excel at
Evaluating trade-offs	Generating solutions
Understanding domain-specific constraints	Retrieving information
Weighing ethical and regulatory factors	Exploring alternatives
Applying creative problem-solving	Spotting patterns across large corporations

Studies on hybrid team dynamics show that human–AI collaboration outperforms either humans alone or AI alone in tasks requiring reasoning, creativity, or exploratory analysis.

Smaller Teams, Bigger Impact

Team Topologies research demonstrates that small, domain-aligned teams with strong boundaries achieve significantly faster flow than large, siloed structures. When these teams are augmented with AI, they become even more potent, as AI systems reduce manual overhead and accelerate discovery. In practice, this augmentation is embedded directly into the team structure. Figure 7.5 illustrates a domain-oriented product team in which engineers focus on higher-value work while AI assistants handle specific mechanical tasks.

Figure 7.5 AI-Augmented Work in a Domain-Aligned Product Team

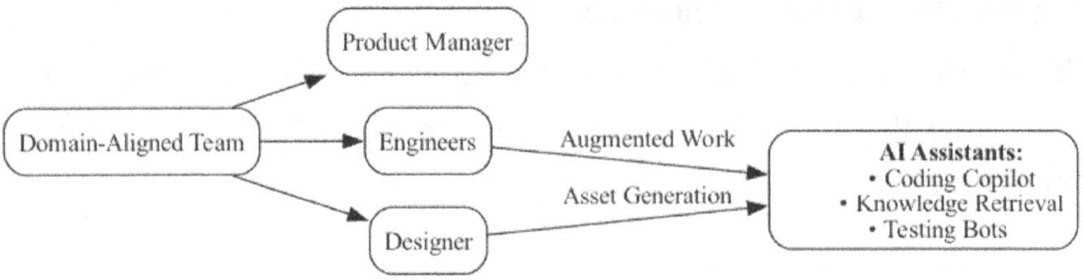

Distributed Knowledge Through AI

AI tools act as continuous knowledge distribution mechanisms. Patterns, conventions, and architectural decisions become immediately accessible to every engineer. Conflux and Team Topologies research both highlight how reducing knowledge bottlenecks increases autonomy and delivery flow [63].

7.4 New Operating Models for Continuous Innovation

To fully leverage AI and modern engineering practices, organizations must adopt operating models built for adaptability, rapid learning, and continuous iteration.

Product-Centric, Domain-Aligned Teams

Long-lived, domain-aligned teams outperform short-term project-based structures. Empirical research consistently shows that stable, empowered teams deliver higher-quality outcomes and maintain better alignment with user needs.

Continuous Decision-Making and Adaptive Planning

The pace of AI-enabled development demands dynamic planning cycles:

- Continuous prioritization

- Rapid experimentation
- Data-driven decisions
- Rolling updates to roadmaps

Continuous software engineering frameworks affirm that responsiveness and tight feedback loops are essential for modern enterprise delivery [2], [7].

AI-Enabled Portfolio Management

AI can analyze user behavior, operational metrics, defect patterns, capacity utilization, and financial impact to support more informed prioritization and investment decisions. This moves enterprise planning toward evidence-based decision-making.

Institutionalizing Experimentation

High-performing organizations embrace continuous experimentation:

- Lightweight A/B tests
- Architectural explorations
- AI-assisted simulations
- Hypothesis-driven development

Such practices are strongly correlated with innovation capability and organizational learning.

7.5 Organizational Transformation Roadmap

Transforming into a future-ready engineering organization requires deliberate changes across culture, structure, process, and technology. Leaders need a deliberate and structured path forward. Figure 7.6 presents a five-phase strategic roadmap that guides organizations from initial assessment through to the institutionalization of new capabilities.

Figure 7.6 Strategic Roadmap for Evolving the Operating Model

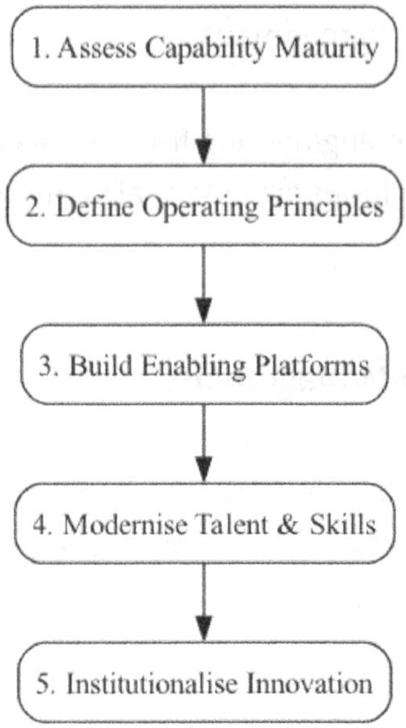

Step 1: Assess Capability Maturity

Leaders must assess:

- Architectural readiness
- Automation coverage
- Platform maturity
- AI adoption patterns
- Governance flexibility

This aligns with Team Topologies and platform engineering recommendations for assessing flow constraints and systemic bottlenecks.

Step 2: Define Future-State Operating Principles

Organizations must articulate principles covering:

- Team autonomy
- Domain boundaries

- AI usage governance
- Golden paths and constraints
- Architectural standards

These principles reduce ambiguity and guide decision-making at scale.

Step 3: Build and Evolve Enabling Platforms

Internal Developer Platforms (IDPs) provide the technical substrate that enables autonomy, safety, and consistency, foundational elements of high-velocity organizations [36].

Step 4: Modernize Talent and Skills

Enterprises should:

- Train teams in prompt engineering
- Develop AI governance playbooks
- Redefine seniority expectations
- Establish AI communities of practice

Workforce evolution research emphasizes upskilling as central to successful hybrid team adoption [60].

Step 5: Institutionalize Continuous Innovation

Enterprises must shift from permission-based governance to guardrail-based governance, allowing teams to experiment safely while maintaining compliance and architectural coherence.

7.6 A Vision for the Enterprise of 2030

The enterprise of 2030 is characterized by:

- Hybrid human–AI delivery teams
- Autonomous pipelines and intelligent platforms

- Composable architectures enabling rapid change
- Domain-aligned product teams
- Continuous experimentation as standard practice
- Pervasive automation of governance and security

These traits function as an integrated and mutually reinforcing system rather than as isolated elements. Figure 7.7 presents this future model as a set of interconnected pillars that together deliver resilience, speed, and autonomy.

Figure 7.7 Foundational Pillars of the Future Enterprise Delivery Model

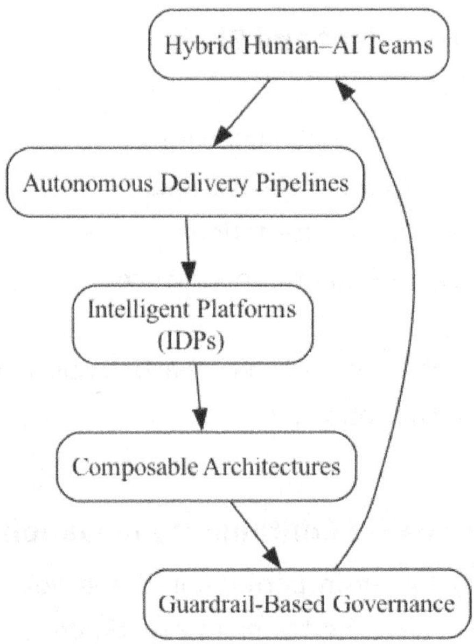

Software becomes a continuously evolving system, shaped collaboratively by engineers and AI. Organizations that adopt these models will differentiate themselves through adaptability, resilience, and innovation capacity. Those that do not will struggle under the weight of complexity, talent constraints, and slow decision cycles.

The next chapter steps from theory into practice. It examines a real-world case study that shows how these principles played out in a complex, regulated environment, and the measurable ROI that resulted from changing the delivery model rather than the ambition.

Chapter 8

Case Study – Project Concord and the ROI

8.1 Case Study Overview

This case study follows a software vendor, referred to here as Vendor Concord (which is not their real name), that set out to develop an enterprise-grade platform to modernize the Aged Care sector globally. The solution was designed to help providers manage governance, regulatory compliance, and operational execution at scale. The product ambition was clear: create a global software product for the Aged Care sector that could replace fragmented processes and disconnected tools across the industry with a single, integrated platform that supports day-to-day operations, drives significant cost reductions for providers, and withstands stringent audit scrutiny and evolving standards.

The initiative began with significant investment and strong intent, but progress was slow under a traditional delivery approach. Over time, Vendor Concord assembled a complete set of user requirements sourced from the market, yet struggled to convert that documentation into a working product at a pace that matched industry urgency and commercial opportunity. At that point, the vendor adopted a new delivery methodology, focused on AI-enabled execution and capability uplift inside the product team rather than relying solely on outsourced build teams.

What makes this case study worth including is not only the end result, but the mechanism: the vendor dramatically changed its delivery economics and speed by changing its operating model. In doing so, it created a repeatable way to deliver enterprise software faster, with less waste, and with better alignment between market needs, product intent, and implementation.

Success, in this case, was defined by three outcomes:

1. Delivering a reliable and scalable working product from an already-defined requirements base
2. Materially reducing the cost and time-to-delivery of the build phase
3. Creating an internal delivery capability that could continue improving the platform and shipping releases after go-live

8.2 Industry Context and Market Pressure

From the vendor's perspective, the Aged Care sector was at an inflection point, where the market's need for an enterprise-grade platform became unavoidable. Expectations were rising on three fronts at once:

- Providers needed stronger operational control,
- Significant operational cost reduction, and
- The ability to prove compliance through evidence rather than intention.

Oversight standards were becoming more demanding, audits were becoming more rigorous, and stakeholders were increasingly expecting real-time transparency rather than periodic reporting.

At the same time, Vendor Concord observed that many providers' operating models were under pressure. Teams were expected to do more with the same headcount, yet critical processes still depended on manual coordination. Work moved across spreadsheets, emails, shared drives, and disconnected systems. The pattern was consistent across organizations: important tasks still got done, but they required heroics, institutional memory, and constant follow-up.

For the vendor, the commercial and product opportunity was clear because the cost of inefficiency in this sector is not only financial. Manual processes increase risk. Fragmented information makes it harder to spot issues early. And when evidence is scattered across systems, audit preparation becomes a scramble rather than a routine outcome of normal operations.

Vendor Concord concluded that incremental tooling would not be enough for the sector. The industry needed a central platform that could standardize workflows, embed governance into the way work was performed, and make compliance an emergent property of daily operations rather than a separate activity done after the fact.

8.3 The Problem to Solve

From the vendor's perspective, the market did not suffer from a single "system failure." It suffered from a systems problem: dozens of small gaps across providers that compounded into significant operational drag, risk, and inconsistency. Operationally, work depended on manual coordination. Information lived in too many places. Updates were shared via email chains and meetings. Reporting required people to chase inputs and reconcile versions. Even when providers were doing the right work, visibility was limited, and progress was hard to measure without additional administrative effort.

For Vendor Concord, governance and compliance were the defining product problems. Providers needed to demonstrate that processes were being followed, that actions were traceable, and that outcomes could be supported with evidence. But when evidence is produced manually, it becomes expensive and unreliable. The industry could not sustainably scale the level of assurance stakeholders expected without changing how work was executed and recorded.

Across the market, this created three common pain points that a credible enterprise-grade solution could solve:

- Administrative overhead was rising
- Skilled staff were spending time on coordination and
- Documentation rather than value-adding work.

Risk was difficult to manage proactively

Issues were often discovered late because data was fragmented and reporting was retrospective.

Audits consumed disproportionate effort

Preparing evidence required concentrated bursts of activity, pulling staff away from core operations.

For Vendor Concord, the implication was clear: the solution could not merely store compliance artefacts. It had to actively shape behavior across provider organizations, guiding users through consistent workflows, capturing evidence as a by-product of work, and making oversight easier for leaders without increasing the administrative burden on the front line.

8.4 The Product Vision

From the vendor's perspective, the goal was never to build "another system." The goal was to create a platform that could become the central operational backbone for Aged Care providers, delivering governance, compliance, and continuous improvement through a single integrated product.

Vendor Concord aimed to deliver Aged Care providers with a single environment that supports frontline execution, leadership oversight, and audit evidence without duplication. In practical product terms, this meant the solution had to do three things exceptionally well.

First, it needed to standardize how work was performed across diverse provider environments. Not by forcing rigid bureaucracy, but by providing clear pathways for common processes, so staff could act consistently even when teams changed, workloads increased, or individual sites operated differently.

Second, it needed to make oversight simple for provider leadership. The product had to deliver visibility into what was happening now, what was overdue, what was trending in the wrong direction, and where risk was accumulating. The intention was to reduce dependence on manual status reporting and give leaders a management view that reflected operational reality.

Third, it needed to be audit-ready by default. Instead of providers collecting evidence as a separate task, the platform needed to capture evidence as work occurred: who did what, when, why, and what outcome was achieved. If a provider were operating properly, the audit story should already exist in the system.

Importantly, Vendor Concord designed the platform around roles, not departments, because the product needed to work across different provider structures. It had to support multiple user types with different needs:

- Operational staff who needed clarity and speed
- Managers who needed visibility and control
- Governance stakeholders who needed traceability and assurance
- Administrators who needed configurable workflows without technical complexity

This vision mattered because it correctly framed the product: it was not a database of compliance artefacts. It was a delivery mechanism for better operations, lower risk, and measurable assurance across the industry.

8.5 Solution Scope and Key Modules

To turn the product vision into something buildable and sellable globally, Vendor Concord translated the platform into a set of capability areas. Each area solved a specific governance and operational problem faced by Aged Care providers, but the design intent was always the same: integrate them so that information flowed naturally, evidence accumulated automatically, and leadership teams could see the full picture without manually assembling it.

Vendor Concord grouped the platform scope into six core modules.

Compliance and standards alignment
A structured way to map obligations, policies, and standards to real operational activities. The goal was to make compliance actionable for providers: not a document that sits on a shelf, but a set of expectations embedded into workflows and measurable through evidence automatically captured in the system.

Governance and reporting

Dashboards and reporting views designed for leadership oversight. This included the ability to track performance, identify overdue actions, and see emerging trends. The focus wasn't reporting for its own sake. It was reporting to isolate problem areas and drive management action within provider organizations.

Incident response and risk

A consistent process for capturing incidents, assessing severity, assigning actions, and tracking resolution. The key requirement was traceability: showing what happened, how it was handled, and what was done to prevent recurrence at both site and organization-wide levels.

Continuous improvement

A way to log improvement opportunities, link them to root causes, assign ownership, and track progress. This module was designed to help providers turn "lessons learned" into an operational habit rather than a periodic review exercise.

Learning and training management

Support for training requirements, completion tracking, and links between competency and operational performance. This closed the loop between what staff were expected to know and what the provider could evidence to regulators and internal governance bodies.

Operational workflows and supporting artefacts

A set of practical workflows that connected the modules together: tasking, approvals, document control, and structured communications. These were deliberately designed as enabling infrastructure, so the platform could scale across multiple facilities without adding administrative workload.

The critical design decision was integration. Each module was valuable on its own, but the commercial differentiation came from how they connected. For example, an incident could trigger corrective actions, link to training needs, drive an improvement initiative, and be automatically reflected in governance reporting. That is the difference between a collection of tools and an enterprise platform.

8.6 Delivery Approach

Vendor Concord initially followed a conventional enterprise product path: gather requirements from the market, validate them with stakeholders, then move into development through a large external build effort. On paper, this sequence appears sensible because it aims to reduce ambiguity before committing to building the product. In practice, it created a long delay between decision and delivery, and that delay became costly in both time-to-market and opportunity cost.

The early phase produced a valuable asset for the vendor: a comprehensive set of user requirements, shaped by real industry needs. But Vendor Concord struggled to translate those requirements into working software. Momentum slowed, confidence declined, and the gap between "what the market needs" and "what users can use today" kept widening.

At this point, Vendor Concord faced a strategic choice. The vendor could proceed with a traditional outsourced delivery model, accepting the high quoted build cost and likely timeline delays. Or it could change the delivery method entirely and adopt an operating model designed to produce working increments quickly, using the requirements as a baseline rather than a finish line.

Vendor Concord chose the second path. The new approach was built around four principles.

Deliver in monthly MVP releases

Instead of waiting for a complete platform, the product team worked in a cadence that produced usable increments. Each release was governed by value delivered in a time-boxed schedule.

Turn requirements into buildable slices

The requirements set remained the source of truth, but it was decomposed into small, testable units that could be built, verified, and refined.

Tight feedback loops with real users

Feedback was gathered from the people doing the work in provider environments, not only from decision-makers and sign-off groups. This ensured the product converged on real operational utility and adoption drivers.

Reduce handover friction

The vendor's goal was to eliminate the typical "business specifies, developers interpret" cycle. The operating model aimed to keep market intent and implementation tightly coupled throughout delivery.

This shift didn't reduce the product ambition. It reduced waste. Vendor Concord stopped measuring progress in artefacts and started measuring progress in working business capability shipped to users.

8.7 AI-Assisted Development in Practice

For Vendor Concord, the turning point was not the decision to "use AI." It was the decision to adopt an AI-enabled product delivery methodology with clear rules, human oversight, and a repeatable workflow that could scale across an enterprise-grade roadmap.

The vendor treated AI as an accelerator across the software lifecycle, not a replacement for product thinking or engineering discipline. The platform still required real architectural decisions, disciplined scope decomposition, and rigorous validation. But once the work was structured correctly, AI materially increased throughput and dramatically reduced time-to-market for core capabilities.

In practice, AI-assisted development was applied in five areas.

1. **Converting requirements into implementation-ready units**
Vendor Concord took the market requirements baseline and broke it into small, buildable slices. Each slice included purpose, user flow, acceptance criteria, edge cases, and test expectations. This mattered because AI output quality rises sharply when inputs are specific and constrained, and because it created a reliable pattern for sprint execution.

2. **Scaffolding the application quickly**
AI was used to generate initial module scaffolding: common patterns, boilerplate code, standard workflows, and repeated UI or API structures. This removed weeks of setup effort that typically consumes early-stage product development and delays first usable releases.

3. **Accelerating iteration and refactoring**
As the platform evolved, AI-supported refactoring consistently proposed improvements and helped reduce technical debt that often accumulates in fast-moving product builds. This allowed the vendor to maintain delivery speed without degrading maintainability.

4. **Expanding test coverage and validation**
AI was used to generate test cases from acceptance criteria and highlight missing cases. Crucially, Vendor Concord did not treat AI-generated tests as complete by default. Tests were reviewed and run as part of a disciplined validation process aligned to enterprise expectations.

5. **Documentation as a by-product, not a project**
User-facing documentation, release notes, and internal technical notes were automatically produced continuously. AI made it feasible for the vendor to keep documentation current without creating a separate documentation effort that competes with feature delivery.

What enabled this work was the human layer. AI created speed, but the product team still had to decide what to build, how to structure it, and how to verify it. Vendor Concord operated with a trust-but-verify stance: every output was validated against acceptance criteria and real usage. In this model, AI compressed effort and increased delivery capacity, while governance and quality remained firmly under the vendor's control.

8.8 Governance, Security, and Audit-Readiness

Because Vendor Concord was building a platform that sits at the center of governance and compliance, it could not treat security and audit-readiness as a late-stage checklist. The product needed to be credible from the first meaningful release, not only after a long hardening phase.

From the vendor's perspective, speed mattered, but speed without control would simply create a new kind of risk for customers and undermine market trust. Vendor Concord, therefore, treated governance and audit-readiness as product qualities that had to grow alongside functionality.

Three principles guided the design and delivery approach.

Governance was designed into the workflow

Rather than relying solely on policy documents and training, Vendor Concord embedded governance into how work moved through the system. Workflows included approvals where needed, required fields where evidence mattered, and structured status transitions so activity could be interpreted reliably across provider environments.

Audit evidence was captured as a by-product of normal work

The platform was designed so that evidence naturally accumulated: what occurred, who performed it, what was approved, and what changed. This reduced reliance on post-hoc reconstruction, which is where audit effort usually becomes expensive for providers.

Guardrails replaced gates

Rather than slowing product delivery and customer onboarding through heavy sign-off cycles, Vendor Concord implemented guardrails that guided appropriate behavior while enabling value-based progress. This included consistent patterns for permissions, repeatable handling of sensitive fields, and disciplined change control around core data structures.

This approach aligned with a broader enterprise lesson: audit-readiness is not an event. It is a product property. If customers need to scramble to prepare for scrutiny, the platform is not doing its job. Vendor Concord aimed to create a solution in which audit preparation is closer to opening the reporting view than to assembling a story from scattered artefacts.

The result was a delivery posture that remained fast but became safer over time. Each release increased capability while also boosting customer confidence, because governance and evidence grew alongside functionality rather than trailing behind it.

8.9 Team Model and Roles

Vendor Concord achieved rapid delivery because its team model aligned with the goal of building an enterprise-grade product quickly while keeping market intent tightly aligned with implementation. Rather than separating “the product business” from “the build,” the vendor relied on a small core team with strong domain understanding, supported by targeted AI enablement.

At the center were two experienced internal staff:

- A Business Analyst who understood the operational reality of Aged Care providers, could express requirements clearly, and could validate outcomes against user needs
- A communications and stakeholder engagement expert who could manage expectations, coordinate feedback, and keep user adoption and product feedback moving

Notably, neither of these roles was a traditional software engineer. In a conventional product build, that would typically lead to a heavy reliance on external development teams and increased translation loss. Under the new AI-enabled methodology, it became an advantage: their strength was clarity of intent and user reality, and the workflow was designed to convert that intent into implementation with minimal distortion.

The enabling role was the key addition: an Enterprise AI Development Coach.

From the vendor's perspective, this coach did not operate as an outsourced development team. The coach's role was to:

- Train the internal staff in the methodology and tools
- Guide decomposition of requirements into buildable increments
- Establish repeatable patterns for quality control, testing, and release cadence
- Provide oversight on architecture and delivery discipline, ensuring speed did not create fragility

The effect of this model was compounding. Rather than buying output once, Vendor Concord bought capability. Each cycle improved the team's ability to deliver, communicate change, and validate outcomes. The team became faster not only because AI reduced effort, but because the operating model reduced confusion, rework, and dependency bottlenecks.

For Vendor Concord, this became a core product lesson: enterprise delivery success is rarely determined by tools alone. It is determined by the combination of roles, workflow, and governance. The vendor improved results by redesigning its delivery system around enablement and iteration, rather than scale and handover.

8.10 Commercial Strategy

From the beginning, Vendor Concord understood that building a large, integrated enterprise platform for the Aged Care sector would be expensive, and that a traditional "big build" would be difficult to fund and de-risk within a single, uninterrupted program of work. The scope was broad, the stakeholder base was large, and the vendor could not afford a multi-year delivery cycle that delivered value only at the end.

The early phase reflected a common enterprise product pattern: invest heavily in definition work to reduce uncertainty before committing to build. That effort produced a complete set of user requirements, but it also consumed a large portion of the budget before meaningful capability reached users, slowing time-to-market.

When Vendor Concord received an expensive development quote, the commercial problem became obvious. Proceeding with a traditional outsourced build meant committing additional capital while still carrying delivery and timeline risks, as well as the familiar risk of misalignment between what was specified and what customers would ultimately adopt.

The alternative strategy was to treat product delivery as an investment engine rather than a one-time capital event. Under the new approach, Vendor Concord shifted to a model with three commercial advantages:

1. **Stage investment against real capability**
   Instead of funding an entire build upfront, investment could be phased in line with measurable value-based delivery. Each increment reduced risk and justified the next.

2. **Convert requirements into release-ready capability sooner**
   Monthly MVP delivery enabled the platform to move toward adoption sooner, shortening the time between spend and customer value.

3. **Reduce reliance on large external delivery teams**
   Vendor Concord didn't eliminate external expertise; it merely focused it. Instead of paying for a full build workforce, it paid for training and enablement that allowed a small internal team to execute with AI acceleration.

This strategy wasn't just about saving money. It improved the quality of investment. Vendor Concord moved from paying for a promise to paying for progress, and that shift directly improved confidence, stakeholder engagement, and the vendor's ability to keep the product roadmap moving fast enough to win market trust.

8.11 ROI and Financial Impact

For Vendor Concord, the ROI story is compelling because it isolates the impact of delivery methodology on cost, speed, and the ability to actually ship an enterprise-grade product. The vendor had already invested heavily before the platform began delivering meaningful capability to the market.

Phase 1: Traditional approach, spend and outcome

Vendor Concord spent $6 million and, while there was little product progress to show in working software, the investment produced one significant asset: a complete set of user requirements derived from industry standards. In other words, the vendor had clarity on what needed to be built but lacked an effective mechanism to turn that clarity into a shipped product.

At this point, the delivery capacity inside the vendor was still limited to two experienced but non-technical roles:

- 1 x Business Analyst
- 1 x Communications and stakeholder engagement expert

To complete the build using a conventional approach, Vendor Concord received several development quotes ranging from $ 1.9 million to $ 2.1 million, in addition to maintaining two internal staff members. This is the point where many software initiatives stall: the team is far enough in to feel committed but facing a new round of spend that still carries timeline risk and product risk.

Phase 2: The new methodology and the economic shift

Instead of accepting the $2.1 million build quote, Vendor Concord adopted a new AI-enabled delivery methodology. The same two internal staff were trained and guided using a structured approach, supported by an Enterprise AI Development Coach who used the methodology described in this book. The coach provided enablement, training, workflow design, decomposition discipline, quality control patterns, and delivery governance.

The result was that Vendor Concord completed the equivalent $2.1 million development scope for $250,000, which was paid to the Enterprise AI Development Coach.

What this means in practical ROI terms:

- Quoted traditional build cost: $2.1m
- Actual cost to complete build under the new model: $250k
- Direct saving on the build component: $1.85m

However, the more important return was structural: Vendor Concord didn't merely buy lower-cost development. It built an internal capability to deliver, iterate, and extend the platform going forward. That means future releases are not priced like a fresh outsourcing engagement. They are delivered through a repeatable operating model with compounding returns.

This is the core economic lesson for enterprise software vendors: the highest ROI often comes not from reducing scope, but from changing the approach and system that converts scope into shipped product.

8.12 Challenges, Lessons Learned, and What Changed

From Vendor Concord's perspective, the program identified a set of challenges common to building enterprise-grade software for a highly regulated industry. What makes this case useful is not that it avoided friction, but that it made clear which issues were structural market realities and which were created by the delivery model itself.

Challenge 1: Requirements did not equal momentum

Vendor Concord had comprehensive requirements, yet delivery still stalled. The lesson was clear: requirements reduce ambiguity, but they do not create a shipped product. Without a delivery system that can convert requirements into validated increments, requirements work becomes an expensive holding pattern, and time-to-market suffers.

Challenge 2: Translation loss between market intent and implementation

In the traditional approach, the vendor followed the familiar chain: users explain needs, analysts document, developers interpret, users review, and rework follows. Each handover introduced ambiguity and interpretation.

The new methodology reduced this translation loss by tightening the loop between what the market needed and what was built, release by release.

Challenge 3: Confidence erosion and stakeholder fatigue

As time passed without a visible product capability, stakeholders became cautious. Customers stop engaging when they feel their input disappears into a nebulous back hole. Once Vendor Concord began releasing monthly MVP value-based increments, confidence recovered because users could see their feedback turning into real functionality.

Challenge 4: Capability gap inside the vendor team

The internal team was strong in analysis and communication, but not in coding. In a conventional build model, this forces dependency on an external development team and increases delivery risk. The AI-enabled delivery approach reframed the gap: instead of outsourcing execution, Vendor Concord invested in enablement, training, and a disciplined workflow, enabling a small internal team to drive delivery with support.

What changed as a result

- Progress became visible because delivery was measured in working business capability shipped to users
- Stakeholders re-engaged because feedback loops were short and meaningful
- Costs fell because the vendor shifted from buying labor to buying methodology and capability
- Quality improved because governance, testing, and documentation became part of the delivery workflow, not a late-stage scramble

The larger lesson for software vendors is that most delivery failure is not caused by insufficient effort. It's caused by a mismatch between the delivery method and the complexity of the product environment. Once

Vendor Concord changed the method, the program became commercially viable and operationally credible.

8.13 Key Takeaways for Executives

For Vendor Concord, the core insight from this case is that enterprise software success is rarely determined by feature ideas alone. It is determined by the delivery machine that turns market needs into shipped capability. The platform mattered, but the decisive advantage came from the operating model used to build it.

1. **Requirements are only valuable when they can be converted into tested releases**
   Comprehensive requirements reduce ambiguity, but they do not create momentum. Vendors should treat requirements as a baseline, then demand a delivery cadence that rapidly turns that baseline into a working, value-based capability.

2. **Delivery economics are driven more by methodology than by scope**
   Vendor Concord did not reduce ambition. It changed how ambition was converted into output. When delivery cost collapses by an order of magnitude, it is rarely a "better deal." It is almost always a different system of work.

3. **AI tools are not the differentiator. The workflow is**
   AI can accelerate scaffolding, iteration, testing, and documentation, but only when work is clearly decomposed and rigorously validated. Vendors that treat AI as a tool purchase will be disappointed. Vendors that adopt AI as a disciplined delivery methodology will see compounding returns.

4. **Enablement beats dependency**
The Enterprise AI Development Coach model worked because it built capability rather than creating ongoing reliance on external teams. Instead of permanently outsourcing delivery, Vendor Concord created an internal engine that can keep delivering after the initial build.

5. **Governance and audit-readiness should be designed in from day one**
If compliance is bolted on at the end, it becomes expensive and fragile. When governance is embedded into workflows and evidence is captured as a by-product, the vendor delivers a product that delivers more customer value and better implementations.

6. **Short release cycles reduce product risk and increase market trust**
Monthly MVP releases changed stakeholder behavior. Visibility increased, engagement returned, and risks were surfaced early. For vendors, the best product risk management often comes down to a tight delivery cadence.

For executives leading enterprise software businesses, the message is straightforward: winning is not only about choosing the right roadmap. It is about building the right delivery machine. Vendor Concord rebuilt that machine mid-flight, and the outcome changed dramatically.

8.14 The Delivery Model Shift

To understand why Vendor Concord's economics changed so dramatically, it helps to describe the shift as a simple comparison of operating models.

In the traditional model, the vendor was operating like this:

- The market defined requirements

- Development was treated as a specialized external activity
- Progress depended on handovers and interpretation
- Value appeared late, after a long build cycle
- Risk accumulated quietly until the end

In the new model, Vendor Concord shifted to this:

- The market still shaped requirements, but the vendor owned execution end-to-end
- Requirements were decomposed into small, testable slices
- AI accelerated implementation, testing, and documentation
- Releases were monthly, so demo-ready value appeared early and often
- Risk was surfaced continuously because each release had to work

The key enabling mechanism was the Enterprise AI Development Coach. For the vendor, this role provided the missing structure: a disciplined workflow, quality controls, reusable patterns, and training that made AI-assisted execution reliable. The coach did not replace the product team. The coach made the team capable of producing software outcomes repeatedly.

In practical terms, Vendor Concord moved from buying an outsourced build to building an internal delivery engine. That is the step-change software executives should pay attention to. Not because it is novel, but because it is repeatable.

8.15 The Case Study Profile Card

Some readers may appreciate a short profile card at the end of a case study. From Vendor Concord's perspective, it reinforces the commercial story, maintains anonymity, and makes the scope and outcome easy to remember.

Vendor type

A software vendor building a global enterprise-grade platform for a highly regulated industry (Aged Care), where evidence, oversight, and compliance are business-critical.

Market drivers observed

- Rising audit and reporting expectations across providers
- Manual administrative load is increasing
- Fragmented tools and inconsistent workflows
- Provider demand for real-time management visibility

Product goal

Deliver a single integrated platform that embeds governance into daily operations, captures evidence automatically, and supports continuous improvement across provider organizations.

Delivery starting point

- $6.0m spent
- Limited working product progress
- Strong asset created: full user requirements baseline derived from industry needs
- Core internal team: Business Analyst + communications/stakeholder expert (non-technical)

Traditional build expectation

- External development quote: $2.1m (additional to internal staff)

New delivery model

- AI-enabled methodology
- Two internal staff trained and guided

- Enterprise AI Development Coach as an enabling role

Outcome (build economics)

- Equivalent $2.1m development scope completed for $250k paid to the coach
- Material reduction in cost and delivery risk
- Internal delivery capability established for ongoing releases and roadmap execution

8.16 Closing: Why This Case Study Matters

From Vendor Concord's perspective, this case study demonstrates a pattern that is becoming unavoidable in enterprise software delivery, especially in regulated industries like Aged Care.

Traditional delivery models assume the main constraints are requirements clarity and funding. This case study showed a different reality: the constraint was the delivery operating model. When the operating model mismatched the complexity of the product environment, even large budgets and clear requirements yielded slow progress and weak time-to-market results.

The most important shift in this case study is that Vendor Concord stopped treating enterprise product delivery as a procurement event and started treating it as an internal capability. By adopting an AI-enabled methodology, supported by targeted advanced AI coaching, the vendor converted a stalled initiative into a working platform and fundamentally changed the economics of shipping enterprise-grade software.

This points to a future direction for enterprise software vendors that need to move faster while remaining credible, compliant, and safe:

- Small teams delivering frequently

- AI as an accelerator, not an authority
- Governance embedded into the workflow
- Building capability is the core investment

Vendor Concord did not just build a platform. It built a repeatable process for building platforms and shipping them to market. And that, more than any feature set, is what will separate high-performing vendors from those trapped in long cycles, high costs, and continual reinvention.

Chapter 9

The Cursor Implementation Playbook

Cursor is a transformative engineering accelerator that can deliver substantial productivity gains when deployed thoughtfully, systematically, and safely. However, achieving consistent, enterprise-grade results requires clear foundations, disciplined workflows, strong governance, and a well-prepared organization. Research across software engineering, AI-assisted development, and human–AI collaboration reinforces these insights, showing that structured adoption patterns significantly reduce risk and improve engineering outcomes[64].

This chapter provides a comprehensive playbook for enterprise leaders seeking to operationalize Cursor at scale.

9.1 Foundational Requirements for Successful Cursor Adoption

High-leverage AI-assisted development requires a strong architectural and organizational foundation. Without these prerequisites, AI tools may amplify technical debt or produce inconsistent, risky outputs[64].

9.2 A Clean, Navigable Codebase

Cursor's multi-file reasoning performs best when the codebase is:

- Modular
- Well-organized
- Consistently styled
- Aligned with clear architectural boundaries

The objective is to evolve from a fragmented codebase into a clean, modular architecture with clearly defined boundaries. Figure 9.1 depicts this essential transformation, demonstrating how it materially improves the accuracy and effectiveness of AI-assisted development.

Figure 9.1 Foundation for AI: From Monolithic to Modular Codebase

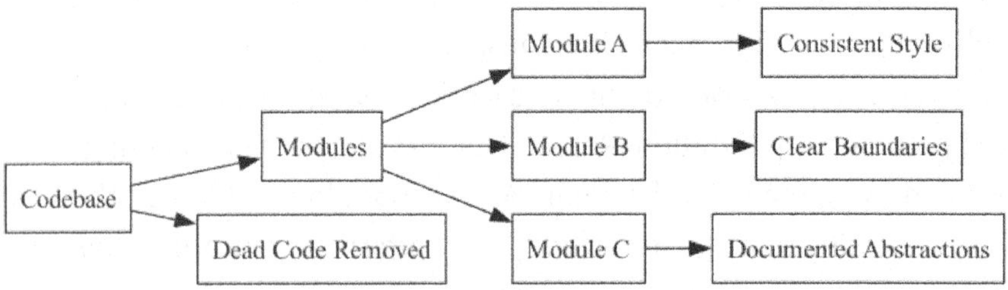

Studies repeatedly show that AI-generated code inherits the structural and stylistic qualities, positive or negative, of the repository it operates within. Organizations should therefore invest in:

- Removing dead code
- Enforcing naming conventions
- Restructuring overly large modules
- Documenting important abstractions

Clean code multiplies AI productivity; messy code multiplies AI errors.

9.3 Platform Engineering and Golden Paths

Internal Developer Platforms (IDPs) provide secure, standardized environments in which AI-generated code can operate reliably. Platform engineering research highlights the value of uniform workflows, standardized infrastructure modules, and paved paths to production, golden paths that reduce ambiguity. When Cursor is used within well-defined workflows, service creation, deployment, testing, and observability, AI output becomes more predictable, maintainable, and compliant with enterprise expectations [65].

9.4 Governance and AI Safety Controls

AI tools must operate within strict enterprise governance. Key controls include:

- Human review requirements
- Approval workflows for large refactors
- Secret-handling and credential safety
- Logging of AI interactions
- Governed model update policies

Well-defined guidelines and controls are required for AI-generated outputs. Figure A.2 conceptualizes this model, showing how compliance and safety are maintained across the entire delivery lifecycle.

Figure 9.2 Governance Model for AI-Generated Output

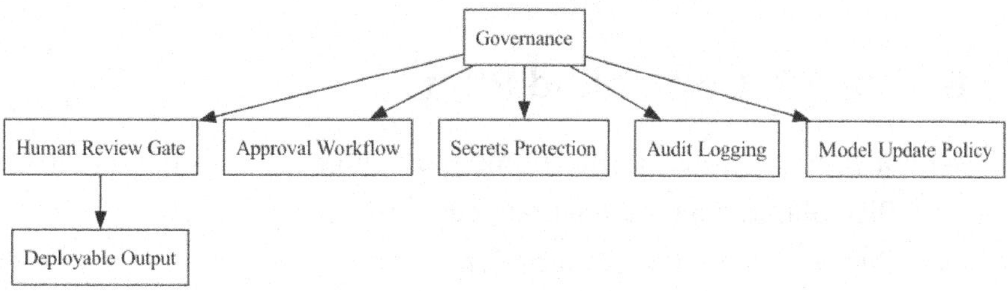

AI safety and human–AI interaction guidelines emphasize the need for clear guardrails, explainability, and predictable model behavior in production environments

9.5 Deployment Strategy: How to Roll Out Cursor Safely and Effectively

Successful organizations adopt Cursor through phased, structured implementation rather than ad hoc experimentation [4], [51], [52]. A disciplined, phased approach is essential for the safe and effective adoption of Cursor. Figure 9.3 presents this roadmap, outlining the progression from controlled experimentation through to full organizational integration.

Figure 9.3 Phased Strategy for Cursor Adoption

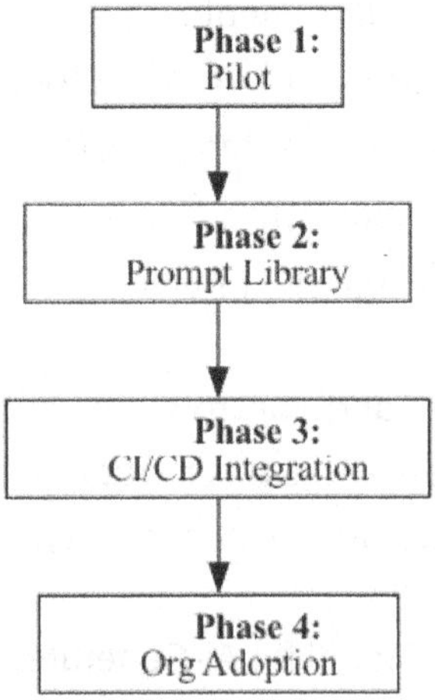

9.6 Phase 1: Controlled Pilot

A pilot should involve a small number of high-capability teams with:

- Disciplined engineering practices
- Strong architectural foundations
- Readiness to provide structured feedback

Pilot teams help identify workflow gaps, governance requirements, and best-fit use cases. Studies on AI-augmented engineering emphasize the importance of pilot environments for calibrating model expectations and developing reusable knowledge[61].

9.7 Phase 2: Prompt Library and Workflow Design

Prompt engineering quality strongly shapes output accuracy. Surveys show that reusable prompt templates significantly improve LLM reliability and reduce hallucinations.

Enterprises should develop:

- Templated prompts for common tasks
- Stepwise decomposition patterns
- Verification prompts ("list assumptions," "explain decisions," "generate test cases")
- Repository-specific contextual prompts

These assets accelerate onboarding and increase consistency across teams.

9.8 Phase 3: Integration with CI/CD and IDPs

AI-generated code must be validated through:

- Automated testing
- SAST and SCA scanners
- Linting and formatting
- Compliance and secrets detection
- Architecture conformance scanning

Research shows that combining AI-assisted generation with automated verification provides the highest code quality and lowest defect rates.

9.9 Phase 4: Organization-Wide Adoption

Once workflows, training materials, and governance policies are stable, organizations can scale Cursor adoption. Large-scale hybrid human–AI collaboration studies show that broad adoption stabilizes once teams share patterns, establish feedback loops, and mature governance mechanisms [62].

9.10 High-Leverage Workflows for Cursor in the Enterprise

Cursor can multiply productivity when aligned with structured development patterns.

9.11 Repository-Wide Refactoring Workflows

Cursor supports repository-wide reasoning, enabling:

- Safe renaming
- Dependency consolidation
- Architectural reshaping
- Service extraction or modularization

These workflows enable a comprehensive transformation cycle, progressing from initial analysis and secure changes through to final validation, as illustrated in Figure 9.4.

Figure 9.4 AI-Assisted Repository Refactoring Workflow

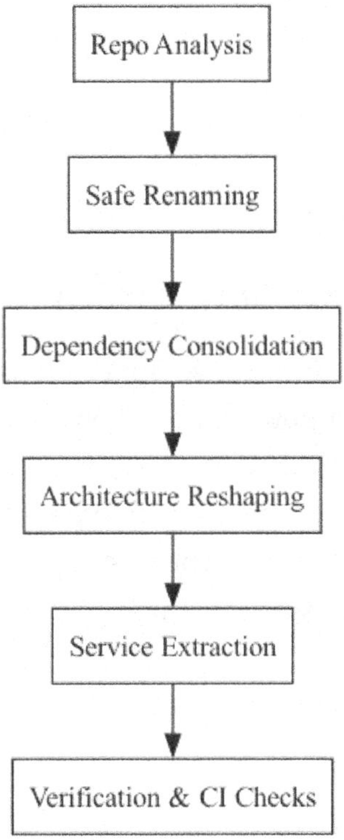

LLM-assisted refactoring research demonstrates substantial time reduction for previously manual, error-prone tasks. When combined with verification prompts and CI-based checks, these workflows deliver both speed and reliability.

9.12 Feature Development with Iterative Prompting

The most effective development pattern follows an iterative loop:

1. Describe intent
2. Request scaffolding
3. Validate

4. Enhance logic
5. Generate tests
6. Integrate

Decomposition improves correctness and reduces hallucination frequency.

9.13 AI-Driven Test Generation

Testing is one of AI's most effective applications. Figure A.5 shows how Cursor can operate as a powerful test-generation engine, transforming code and complex scenarios into a comprehensive suite of automated tests. Studies demonstrate that AI-generated tests significantly improve coverage, uncover defects that might otherwise be missed, and accelerate the creation of regression suites. [57].

Figure 9.5 AI-Powered Test Generation Process

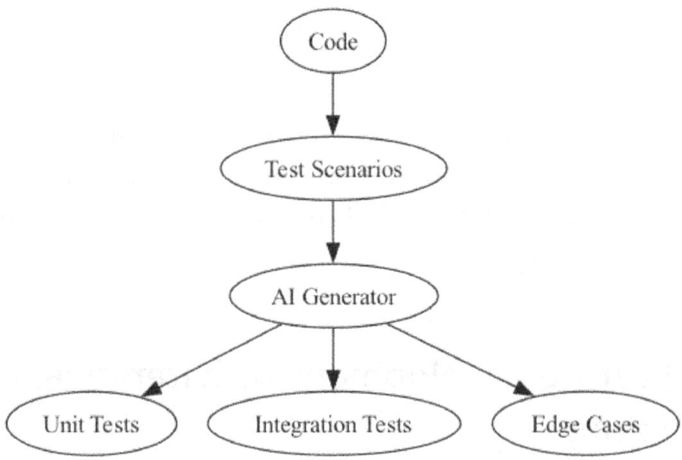

Cursor can generate:

- Unit tests
- Integration tests

- Edge-case scenarios
- Behavioral tests

9.14 Debugging and Root-Cause Assistance

Cursor can assist by:

- Interpreting stack traces
- Summarizing logs
- Identifying logic inconsistencies
- Proposing remediation strategies

Research shows that AI-assisted debugging reduces cognitive load and accelerates time-to-resolution.

9.15 Documentation on Demand

Cursor can generate:

- API documentation
- Architecture diagrams
- Codebase summaries
- Onboarding guides

Documentation production is traditionally a major bottleneck; when it becomes nearly effortless, it improves long-term maintainability.

9.16 Reducing Hallucinations and Ensuring Reliability at Scale

Hallucinations cannot be completely removed, but their likelihood and impact can be effectively managed through disciplined workflows. Figure 9.6 outlines this structured approach to AI interaction, highlighting incremental progress, strong contextual grounding, and systematic verification to ensure reliable outcomes.

Figure 9.6 Framework for Reliable AI-Assisted Development

9.17 Work in Small, Verifiable Steps

Breaking tasks into micro-increments consistently increases output accuracy, as demonstrated in multiple studies on LLM reasoning and decomposition [52].

9.18 Provide Grounding Data

Grounding the model with:

- Existing code
- Style guides
- Architecture boundaries
- Domain rules

Significantly reduces hallucinated logic paths.

9.19 Use Verification Prompts Aggressively

Verification prompts help AI systems detect their own errors. Research in AI-powered software testing shows strong performance when verification is explicitly requested [3].

9.20 Enforce Automated Quality Gates

CI/CD and IDP enforcement ensure:

- Security compliance
- Architectural integrity
- Consistency
- Reproducibility

Studies across AI-assisted engineering stress that automated controls are essential for managing risk at scale. Automation can minimize compliance bottlenecks, improve security, and enhance overall efficiency in modern software development pipelines [66].

9.21 Training and Upskilling for AI-Augmented Teams

A successful AI transformation depends on human capability.

9.22 Core Skills Developers Must Learn

Engineers must acquire skills in:

- Prompt engineering
- Decomposition
- AI failure-mode identification
- Architectural alignment
- Verification and governance

Research confirms that human–AI hybrid performance improves dramatically when teams develop these skills explicitly [5].

9.23 Recommended Training Pathway

Training should proceed in stages:

1. Fundamentals of AI-assisted development
2. Prompt design and decomposition
3. Multi-stage workflows
4. Collaborative reasoning with Cursor

5. Verification techniques
6. Repository-scale transformations
7. Secure and compliant AI usage

AI-augmented engineering should evolve through increasingly advanced levels of capability. Figure 9.7 illustrates this maturity pathway, showing how organizations build from foundational skills toward large-scale transformation capacity.

Figure 9.7 AI-Augmented Engineering Skills Maturity Pathway

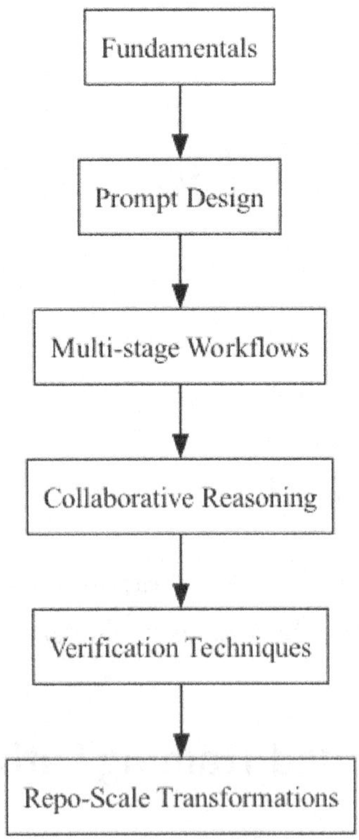

9.24 Communities of Practice

Communities improve adoption by enabling:

- Shared prompt libraries
- Discussion of failures and refinements
- Propagation of best practices
- Feedback to platform and architecture teams

Knowledge-sharing structures are strongly correlated with the successful adoption of hybrid human–AI workflows [65].

9.25 Measuring Success: Metrics for AI-Accelerated Engineering

Delivery leaders should track:

- Cycle time
- Code review throughput
- Defect escape rate
- Onboarding duration
- Architectural consistency
- Developer sentiment

Continuous software engineering research emphasizes that metrics-driven adaptation increases the likelihood of successful operating model transformation [11].

9.26 The Strategic Role of Cursor in the Future Enterprise

Cursor is not just an IDE or productivity tool; it is a foundational capability for modern enterprise software development. When integrated with platform engineering, clean architecture, robust governance, and continuous experimentation, it enables:

- Higher developer throughput
- Lower cognitive load
- Rapid onboarding
- Improved quality
- Faster innovation cycles

Industry research indicates that hybrid human-AI teams deliver superior results compared to fully manual workflows, especially in complex software delivery environments. Cursor enables organizations to reach these future operating models years ahead of competitors.

Chapter 10

Design Patterns and Anti-Patterns for AI-Augmented Engineering

As AI becomes embedded across the software development lifecycle, engineers must adopt new patterns to ensure accuracy, maintainability, and long-term system health. LLMs introduce powerful capabilities, repository-wide reasoning, multi-step code generation, automated refactoring, but they also introduce new risks, including hallucinations, architectural drift, and overfitting to inconsistent patterns. Emerging research across software engineering, HCI, and AI-assisted development identifies recurring success patterns and predictable failure modes in hybrid human–AI workflows[4]. This appendix presents a set of design patterns and anti-patterns that enable teams to use AI development tools safely, reliably, and strategically within enterprise environments.

10.1 Foundational Design Patterns for AI-Assisted Engineering

Effective AI-augmented engineering relies on several foundational design patterns that substantially improve output quality and consistency.

10.2 The Decomposition Pattern

Research demonstrates that large tasks dramatically increase hallucination risk and reduce LLM reasoning quality [5].

Therefore, complex work should be decomposed into:

- Small, atomic prompts
- Sequential steps
- Verifiable intermediate outputs

Example workflow:

1. Generate scaffolding
2. Implement core logic
3. Add error handling
4. Create tests
5. Document behavior

This pattern consistently produces higher-quality results than monolithic prompting.

Figure 10.1 illustrates this methodical approach, which ensures clarity and lowers the risk of hallucinations by breaking down a difficult task into smaller, verifiable steps.

Figure 10.1 Decomposition Pattern for AI-Assisted Development

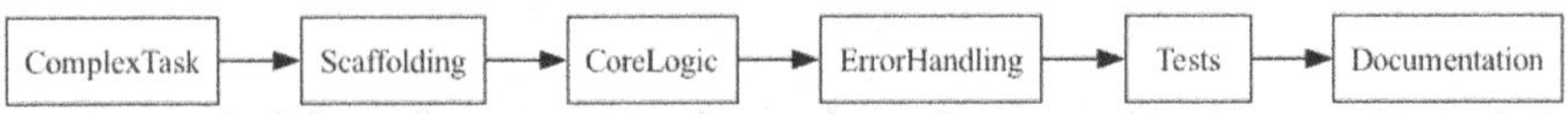

10.3 The Grounded Prompt Pattern

Grounding improves accuracy by anchoring the model in real code, existing architecture, and known behaviors.

Grounding sources include:

- Explicit file references
- Existing functions
- Documented constraints
- Architecture diagrams

Studies show that grounded LLM prompts reduce hallucinations and improve semantic alignment with the codebase.

10.4 The Iterative Enhancement Pattern

LLMs excel when used as iterative collaborators.

The pattern is:

1. Generate a first draft
2. Critique the draft
3. Request improvements
4. Validate and refine

This iterative loop mirrors human pair-programming, and experiments show it outperforms single-pass generation for correctness and readability.

10.5 The Bidirectional Verification Pattern

This pattern asks the model to:

- Justify its reasoning
- List assumptions

- Identify potential bugs
- Propose test cases

AI self-verification significantly increases reliability and exposes erroneous logic early.

This pattern should become standard practice for all AI-generated code. Figure 10.2 shows the verification loop used to rigorously validate AI-generated outputs through test case generation, assumption checking, and justification.

Figure 10.2 Bidirectional Verification Workflow

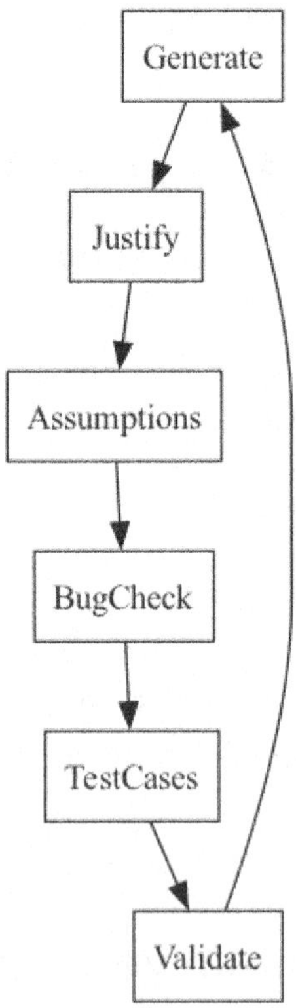

10.6 The Pattern Injection Technique

LLMs replicate patterns they observe. By injecting architectural patterns or examples:

- Domain-driven aggregates
- Repository interfaces
- Middleware templates
- Naming standards

Developers can guide the AI toward correct structures.

Research confirms that example-driven prompting (few-shot prompting) increases consistency and reduces structural defects. The LLM is guided to produce coordinated, architecturally compatible outputs in response to canonical examples and constraints, as shown in Figure 10.3.

Figure 10.3 Pattern-Aligned Prompting with Constraints

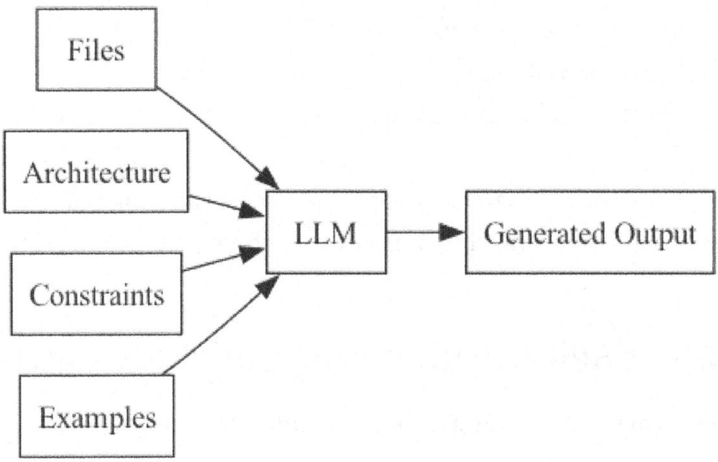

10.7 The Multi-File Diff Pattern

Cursor's multi-file awareness allows complex changes to be applied across a repository in a single coordinated operation.

This pattern:

- Reduces human coordination
- Prevents drift
- Enforces consistency across modules

Large-scale LLM refactoring studies show this pattern is essential for correctness and coherence in multi-file transformations.

10.8 Architecture-Level Design Patterns for AI-Compatible Systems

AI works best in systems that are modular, explicit, and well-structured.

10.9 The Clear-Boundaries Pattern

AI produces more accurate output when modules have:

- Single responsibilities
- Well-defined interfaces
- Explicit domain boundaries

This aligns with research on continuous software engineering, which emphasizes architectural clarity as key to high-velocity change[5].

10.10 The Self-Documenting Codebase Pattern

LLMs perform better in codebases where information is:

- Obvious
- Consistent
- Easy to infer

Self-documenting conventions: clear variable names, concise modules, and consistent patterns enable more accurate multi-step reasoning .

10.11 The Golden Path Conformance Pattern

When AI tools operate within defined golden paths, they:

- Reduce error rates
- Produce compliant code
- Avoid architectural drift

Platform engineering findings show that consistent workflows improve predictability and reduce cognitive load for both humans and AI[55].

10.12 The Canonical Example Pattern

Include authoritative examples of:

- API style
- controller patterns
- testing structures
- data validation approaches

LLMs gravitate toward these examples, making them powerful tools for architectural enforcement [67].

10.13 Anti-Patterns That Increase Risk and Reduce Quality

Several recurring anti-patterns consistently degrade AI output or create long-term maintainability issues.

10.14 The Mega-Prompt Anti-Pattern

Large, ambiguous prompts lead to:

- Hallucinated logic
- Misunderstood requirements
- Incorrect architectural assumptions

Studies confirm a direct correlation between prompt size and error likelihood.

10.15 The Context Starvation Anti-Pattern

If AI is not provided with:

- Relevant files
- Examples
- Architectural constraints

It will invent plausible-sounding but incorrect implementations. This anti-pattern contributes heavily to hallucinations.

10.16 The Copy-Paste Overreliance Anti-Pattern

Blindly accepting AI output:

- Increases defect density
- Reduces architectural coherence
- Introduces security vulnerabilities

Research shows LLMs sometimes generate insecure patterns unless corrected through strict validation [66].

10.17 The Silent Drift Anti-Pattern

When AI repeatedly modifies code without architectural anchoring, systems drift from intended design.

This occurs when:

- Boundaries are blurry
- Patterns are inconsistent
- No ADRs or conventions exist

Architectural drift is a well-documented outcome of undisciplined refactoring.

10.18 The Non-Iterative Prompt Anti-Pattern

Single-shot prompts rarely yield high-quality code. Without iterative feedback loops, accuracy, readability, and maintainability degrade.

10.19 The Governance Bypass Anti-Pattern

Allowing AI-generated code to bypass:

- Code review
- Automated testing
- Security scanning
- Architectural validation

creates systemic risk. Strong AI governance frameworks emphasize that AI output must pass the same or stricter controls as human code. By leveraging tools such as Open Policy Agent (OPA), OWASP ZAP, and Terraform, the framework integrates real-time compliance checks directly into the development workflow. This approach ensures consistent regulatory adherence, reduces reliance on manual processes, and accelerates software delivery [66].

10.20 Patterns for AI-Assisted Refactoring and Modernization

Refactoring is one of AI's highest-value use cases.

10.21 The Guided Refactor Pattern

The human designer provides:

- High-level intent
- Constraints
- Staged steps
- Acceptance criteria

LLM performs the mechanical work; humans provide strategic direction. This pattern is validated in empirical multi-file refactoring studies [54]. AI-assisted refactoring follows a staged pipeline, as illustrated in Figure 10.4, ensuring a safe and methodical transformation from structuring and core algorithms to error handling and validation.

Figure 10.4 Staged AI-Assisted Refactoring Pipeline

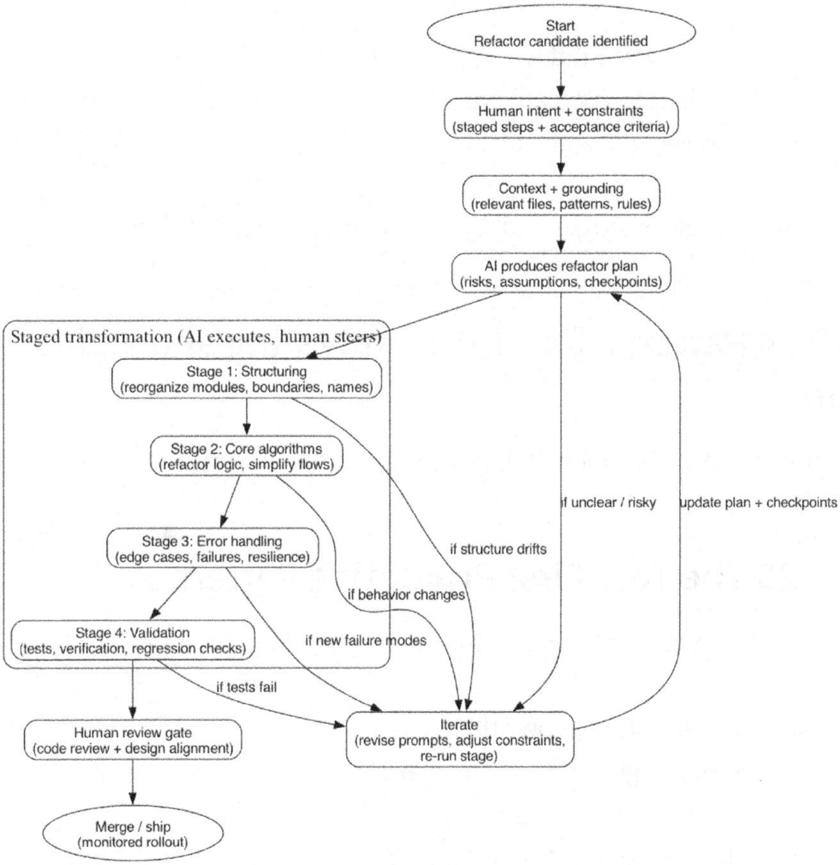

10.22 The "Explain, Modify, Verify" Cycle

1. Ask Cursor to explain a subsystem
2. Request a guided modification
3. Perform bidirectional verification

This pattern improves understanding while reducing the cognitive load of reasoning across a large system.

10.23 The Semantic Diff Pattern

Have Cursor:

- Explain why a diff was generated
- Identify downstream impacts
- Propose additional tests

This strengthens trust and reduces unintended side effects.

10.24 Patterns for AI-Driven Testing and Validation

Testing is essential when AI participates in code generation.

10.25 The Test-First Prompting Pattern

Ask Cursor to generate tests **before** writing the implementation.

AI testing literature shows this:

- Detects logical inconsistencies early
- Clarifies requirements
- Improves generative accuracy[56].

This test-driven strategy is illustrated in Figure 10.5, where AI generates test cases before implementation to ensure that requirements are understood and flaws are identified early.

Figure 10.5 Test-First AI Prompting Workflow

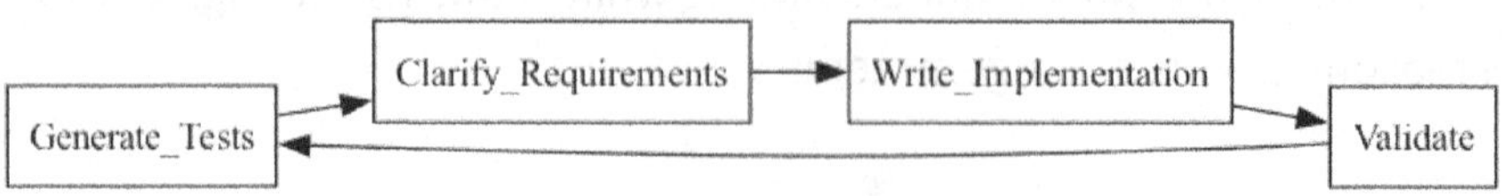

10.26 The Edge-Case Enumeration Pattern

Prompt Cursor to list:

- Edge cases
- Invalid inputs
- Boundary conditions

This aligns with research showing LLMs identify many cases humans overlook [68].

10.27 The Regression Shield Pattern

Automatically run:

- AI-generated tests
- Human-reviewed tests
- Coverage analysis

As a safeguard against hallucination-induced regressions. A dependable feedback loop that minimizes drift and reinforces correct patterns is created by standard examples and aligned outputs, as shown in Figure 10.6.

Figure 10.6 Canonical Example-Driven AI Alignment

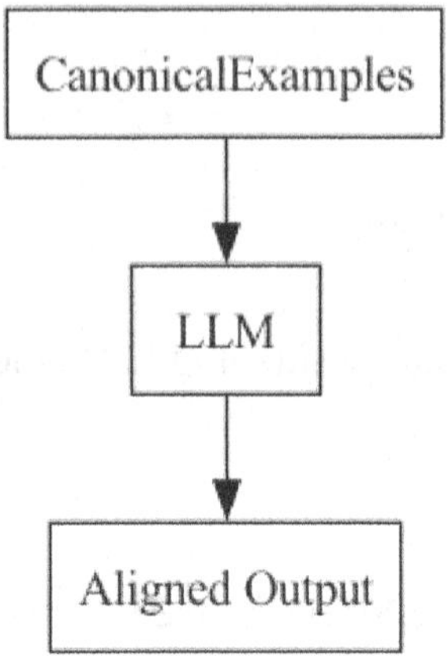

10.28 Patterns for Documentation and Knowledge Transfer

Documentation remains one of AI's most valuable contributions.

10.29 The Layered Summarization Pattern

Cursor can generate:

- High-level summaries
- Module-level summaries
- Function-level explanations

This layered approach mirrors cognitive science principles for knowledge transfer and accelerates onboarding.

10.30 The Architecture Narrative Pattern

Ask Cursor to produce:

- Domain diagrams
- Integration explanations
- Sequence flows

LLM summarization research indicates that AI excels at pattern extraction from large corporations [68].

10.31 Strategic Guidance for Embedding These Patterns Organization-Wide

To ensure consistent adoption, organizations should:

- Maintain a shared pattern library
- Embed patterns in training programs
- Integrate patterns into platform workflows
- Reinforce patterns through code review
- Automate quality gates aligned with patterns

Human–AI collaboration studies show that institutionalizing patterns dramatically improves reliability and performance across teams [61]. Lastly, Figure 10.7 presents an organizational framework that combines staged steps, AI restructuring, human intent, and review cycles to ensure safe and flexible adoption.

Figure 10.7 Governance Model for AI-Augmented Engineering

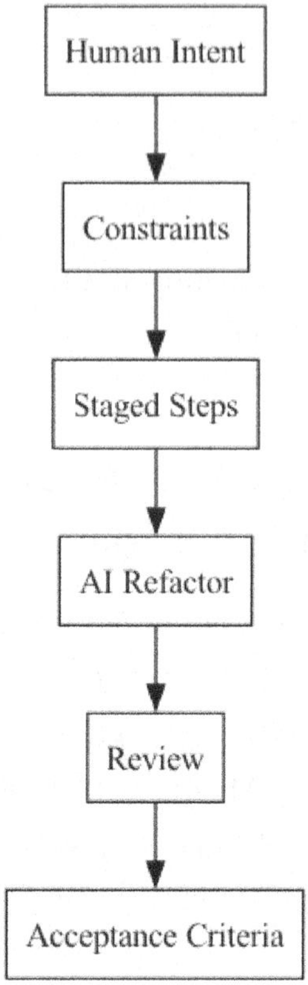

Conclusion: The Future of Enterprise Software Delivery

Enterprise software delivery is entering a new epoch defined by unprecedented levels of intelligence, automation, and adaptability. Cloud-native architectures, platform engineering, AI-augmented development environments, and continuous governance mechanisms are collectively reshaping not only how software is built, but how organizations think, operate, and compete. The transformation described throughout this book is not a mere evolution of tools or methodologies; it represents a foundational reconfiguration of the digital enterprise.

At the center of this shift lies a movement from manual delivery to increasingly autonomous, adaptive systems.

Modern software is no longer a static asset built through discrete phases of design, implementation, and release. Instead, it has become a living, evolving organism, one that learns from operational feedback, adapts to user behavior, self-optimizes its performance, and continuously improves its reliability and security. The rise of AI-enabled delivery pipelines, self-remediating infrastructure, and intelligent developer platforms is accelerating this transition, enabling software ecosystems that respond fluidly to emerging conditions. Studies across engineering and organizational science consistently show that high-performing enterprises embrace these adaptive patterns earlier and more effectively than their peers, positioning themselves for sustained advantage in dynamically shifting markets.

While technology provides the foundation, the most consequential transformation is cognitive. The relationship between human engineers and software systems is fundamentally changing. Engineers are increasingly supported by AI partners capable of reading entire repositories, generating code, anticipating system interactions, and performing complex refactoring. In this hybrid mode of working, AI expands the mental bandwidth of developers, while developers provide strategic judgment, architectural insight, domain understanding, and ethical reasoning. Emerging studies on human–AI collaboration demonstrate that hybrid teams outperform either humans or AI alone in tasks requiring creativity, critical thinking, and multi-step reasoning. The future of engineering belongs to those who can orchestrate this partnership effectively, turning AI into a meaningful extension of human capability rather than a mere tool.

To realize this potential, organizations must adopt operating models designed for flexibility, speed, and continuous renewal. Traditional structures centered on functional silos, sequential delivery processes, and heavyweight governance models cannot support the pace or complexity of modern digital ecosystems. Instead, enterprises must organize themselves around domain-aligned, long-lived product teams that possess both autonomy and responsibility for delivering ongoing customer and business outcomes. These teams operate within environments shaped by platform engineering, which provides consistent pathways for building, testing, deploying, and securing software while reducing cognitive load and variation. Research on software flow and team design shows that such models significantly outperform traditional structures, especially when combined with clear architectural boundaries, strong feedback loops, and high levels of technical automation.

As AI becomes increasingly embedded into delivery ecosystems, the need for robust ethical and governance frameworks grows correspondingly. Organizations must ensure that AI-driven systems operate transparently, securely, and responsibly. This requires clear policies governing model behavior, oversight mechanisms for detecting and mitigating hallucinations, and compliance structures that align with emerging regulations such as the European Union's AI Act [70]. These responsibilities extend beyond technical concerns. They encompass fundamental questions about trust, accountability, and the role of human judgment in automated systems. Leadership teams must cultivate a culture that embraces AI's power while respecting its limitations, maintaining human oversight as the ultimate arbiter of system behavior.

Looking toward 2035, enterprise software delivery will be defined by systems that are significantly more autonomous, intelligent, and capable of self-management. Development teams will be smaller but more skilled, operating with amplified capacity through AI co-engineers. Architectures will be more modular and composable, allowing organizations to reconfigure systems rapidly in response to market shifts. AI-enabled developer platforms will orchestrate much of the delivery workflow, guiding engineers through safe, efficient, and compliant pathways. Innovation cycles will accelerate dramatically, powered by AI-assisted ideation, rapid prototyping, automated refactoring, and continuous experimentation. In this environment, human roles will increasingly center on strategic decision-making, creative problem-solving, and stewardship of ethical and responsible AI practices.

Ultimately, the future of enterprise software delivery is a call to leadership. Organizations that invest in modern architectures, platform foundations, AI-augmented delivery systems, and talent transformation will not merely improve efficiency; they will unlock new forms of competitive advantage, operational resilience, and innovation capacity. Those that delay will face increasing levels of technical and strategic debt in a world where adaptability is the primary currency of success.

The path forward is clear. The tools exist. The models have been validated. The opportunity is immense. It now falls to today's leaders, architects, engineers, and innovators to build the next era of software delivery, one defined not by its constraints, but by its unprecedented potential.

Glossary

AI-augmented engineering
An approach to software delivery where AI systems participate in engineering work (for example, code generation, test creation, analysis, and refactoring) while humans provide intent, constraints, review, and accountability.

AI-driven risk scoring
Using AI to estimate the risk of a change introducing defects or vulnerabilities based on signals such as code history, dependencies, and complexity, and adjusting delivery actions accordingly.

AI-enabled development environment
A development environment that uses AI to understand and operate across a codebase, helping engineers generate, modify, explain, and refactor code with repository context. The manuscript uses Cursor as a prime example.

AIOps
AI-assisted operations that analyze logs, metrics, and traces to detect anomalies, reduce alert noise, support root-cause analysis, and enable faster or automated remediation.

Architectural drift
A gradual divergence from the intended architecture due to incremental changes over time, often driven by inconsistent patterns, unclear boundaries, or undisciplined refactoring.

Architectural technical debt

Structural compromises or accumulated design issues that increase long-term cost of change, reduce delivery speed, and often require refactoring or redesign to resolve.

Autonomous delivery pipelines

Delivery pipelines that go beyond scripted automation by making context-aware decisions (for example, test selection, deployment strategy, roll-back triggers) based on signals from code, policy, and production behavior. The manuscript also frames this as an evolution toward cognitive DevOps.

Change failure rate

The proportion of changes that result in incidents, rollbacks, or degraded service, reflecting release quality and stability.

CI/CD

Automated practices and pipelines that integrate changes frequently and deliver or deploy them reliably through build, test, and release automation.

Cloud-native architecture

Architecture designed for modern cloud environments, favoring scalability, resilience, and rapid change through patterns such as containers, microservices, and elastic infrastructure.

Compliance as code

Automating compliance validation and evidence collection through pipelines, logs, and platform controls so compliance is continuously demonstrable rather than periodic.

Co-engineer model

A working model where AI acts as an engineering partner that produces drafts and explores options, while the human directs the work through decomposition, constraints, verification, and architectural judgement.

Cognitive load

The mental overhead required to understand systems, tools, and dependencies in order to deliver changes; higher cognitive load tends to reduce throughput and increase errors.

Composable architecture

An architecture approach where systems are assembled from modular components that can be independently evolved, replaced, or scaled, improving agility and reducing the cost of change.

Continuous delivery

A delivery approach where software is kept in a deployable state through automation and fast feedback, enabling frequent releases with controlled risk.

Continuous verification

Ongoing automated validation that code, infrastructure, and runtime behavior conform to security and governance requirements as systems change.

DORA metrics

A widely used set of delivery performance measures: deployment frequency, lead time for changes, change failure rate, and mean time to recovery.

Deployment frequency

How often changes are deployed to production over a given period, used as an indicator of delivery throughput.

Developer experience (DevEx)
The ease and effectiveness of the day-to-day developer workflow, influenced by friction, context switching, tooling coherence, and how quickly teams can ship changes.

DevSecOps 2.0
A more mature DevSecOps model where security is embedded deeply into the lifecycle with automation, continuous controls, and platform guardrails rather than manual approvals.

Golden paths
Opinionated, well-supported workflows (also called paved paths) that encode best practices and compliance so teams can move quickly with consistent, safe outcomes.

Guardrails vs gates
A governance shift from blocking approvals and manual checkpoints (gates) to enabling safe autonomy through automated constraints, templates, and continuous checks (guardrails).

Hallucinations (LLMs)
A failure mode where an AI model produces confident, plausible output that is incorrect, unsafe, or misaligned with the actual codebase, requirements, or constraints.

Human–AI hybrid team
A team operating mode where humans and AI systems complement each other: AI increases speed and reduces repetitive work; humans contribute domain understanding, design trade-offs, governance, and validation.

Internal Developer Platform (IDP)
A self-service platform that provides standardized, governed workflows for building, deploying, and operating software (including CI/CD, provisioning, security, observability, and compliance), often delivered through golden paths and developer-facing interfaces.

Lead time for changes
The time it takes for a code change to move from commit to running in production, reflecting the delivery flow speed.

LLM-assisted refactoring
Using AI to speed up structural code changes across one or many files, typically guided by staged prompts and verified through reviews and automated tests to avoid regressions or drift.

Mean time to recovery (MTTR)
The average time required to restore service after an incident, reflecting operational resilience and response effectiveness.

Microservices
An architectural style where functionality is delivered through independently deployable services, improving scalability and fault isolation while increasing distributed-system complexity.

Modular architecture
A design approach that separates responsibilities into clear components with explicit boundaries to reduce coupling and make change easier and safer.

Monolithic architecture
An architecture where major functionality is delivered as a single tightly coupled unit, often increasing the cost and risk of change as the system grows.

Packaged Business Capabilities (PBCs)
Modular components aligned to a specific business domain (such as payments or onboarding) that can be combined to form broader enterprise systems.

Platform engineering
A discipline focused on building internal platforms as products, standardising workflows and tooling to reduce friction and cognitive load while enabling teams to deliver software safely and quickly.

Policy as code
Representing governance and compliance rules in machine-enforceable form so systems can automatically validate and enforce them continuously, especially in pipelines and platforms.

Prompt engineering
The practice of designing prompts and workflows that reliably direct AI systems, typically using decomposition, explicit constraints, examples, and iterative refinement.

Repository-wide reasoning
An AI capability to understand and reason across many files, dependencies, and system context (often called multi-file reasoning), enabling coherent changes that span a codebase.

Security as code
Embedding security controls and checks into templates and automated workflows so security becomes a continuous property of delivery rather than a manual review step.

Self-service provisioning

A capability that allows teams to create and manage environments and resources through standard, automated workflows rather than manual operational processes.

Verification

A discipline of validating AI-generated outputs by surfacing assumptions, checking reasoning, generating tests, and using automated quality gates (tests, scanners, linters) so generated work is trustworthy.

Zero Trust

A security model that assumes no implicit trust and instead relies on identity-centric access control, least privilege, and continuous verification of access and behaviour.

References

[1] S. Anasuri and G. P. Rusum, “AI-Driven Software Design Patterns: Automation in System Architecture,” 2023.

[2] A. Shaheen, M. Al Khaldy, W. Alzyadat, and A. Alhroob, “AI-Driven Augmented Software Engineering: Leveraging Cognitive Models for Enhanced Code Generation,” *J. Comput. Cogn. Eng.*, Nov. 2025, doi: 10.47852/bonviewJCCE52026123.

[3] C.; M. Bird S.;. Barr, E., “The impact of AI on developer productivity: Evidence from GitHub Copilot,” *arXiv*, 2023.

[4] M. Alenezi and M. Akour, “AI-Driven innovations in software engineering: A review of current practices and future directions,” *Appl. Sci.*, vol. 15, no. 3, p. 26, 2024, doi: https://doi.org/10.3390/app15031344.

[5] H. Woo and Y. Cho, “Human-AI Collaboration; Students Changing Perceptions of Generative Artificial Intelligence and Active Learning Strategies,” *Sustainability*, vol. 17, no. 18, p. 22, 2025, doi: 10.3390/su17188387.

[6] The Linux Foundation, “2024 Cloud Native Security Report,” Cloud Native Computing Foundation, USA, Industry research report Not numbered, 2024. Accessed: Dec. 15, 2025. [Online]. Available: https://www.linuxfoundation.org/hubfs/Research%20Reports/lfr_cloudnative_security24_101424a.pdf

[7] A. I. Daraojimba, “Systematic review of key performance metrics in modern DevOps and software reliability engineering,” *Int. J. Future Eng. Innov.*, vol. 1, no. 1, p. 7, 2024, doi: https://doi.org/10.54660/IJFEI.2024.1.1.101-107.

[8] O. T. Murire, “Artificial Intelligence and Its Role in Shaping Organizational Work Practices and Culture,” *Adm. Sci.*, vol. 14, no. 12, p. 316, Nov. 2024, doi: 10.3390/admsci14120316.

[9] DORA Research Group, "Accelerate: State of DevOps 2024 Report," Google/DORA, USA, Research report Not assigned, 2024. Accessed: Dec. 09, 2025. [Online]. Available: https://services.google.com/fh/files/misc/2024_final_dora_report.pdf

[10] N. Forsgren, *J. Humble and G. Kim*. Accelerate: The Science of Lean Software and DevOps, 2018.

[11] B. Fitzgerald and K. J. Stol, "Continuous software engineering and beyond: trends and challenges," in *Proceedings of the 1st International Workshop on Rapid Continuous Software Engineering (RCoSE 2014)*, in RCoSE 2014 Workshop Proceedings, vol. Single book. Hyderabad, India: Association for Computing Machinery (ACM), 2014, p. 9. doi: 10.1145/2593812.2593813.

[12] B. Fitzgerald and K. J. Stol, "Continuous software engineering: A roadmap and agenda," *J. Syst. Softw.*, vol. 123, no. Not separately numbered, p. 189, 2015, doi: 10.1016/j.jss.2015.06.063.

[13] R. Amaro, R. Pereira, and M. M. D. Silva, "Mapping DevOps capabilities to the software life cycle: A systematic literature review," *Inf. Softw. Technol.*, vol. 177, no. NA, p. 25, 2024, doi: 10.1016/j.infsof.2024.107583.

[14] F. Erich, C. Amrit, and M. Daneva, "A mapping study on cooperation between information system development and operations," *Prod. Focus. Softw. Process Improv. PROFES 2014*, vol. 8892, no. Conference proceedings, p. 280, 2017, doi: https://doi.org/10.1007/978-3-319-13835-0_21.

[15] M. E. Misri, "The impact of DevOps practices on software development lifecycle," *Int. J. Creat. Res. Thoughts*, vol. 12, no. 12, p. 8, 2024, doi: https://ijcrt.org/papers/IJCRT2412276.pdf.

[16] J. Fritzsch, J. Bogner, A. Zimmermann, and S. Wagner, "Challenges of microservices architecture: A survey on the state of the practice," 2018.

[17] M. Shahin, "Continuous Integration, Delivery and Deployment: A Systematic Review," *IEEE Access*, vol. 5, no. NA, p. 32, 2017, doi: 10.1109/ACCESS.2017.2685629.

[18] S. Kansal and V. S. Balasubramaniam, "Microservices Architecture in Large-Scale Distributed Systems: Performance and Efficiency Gains," no. 4.

[19] A. Ziegler *et al.*, "Measuring GitHub Copilot's impact on productivity," *Commun. ACM*, vol. 67, no. 3, p. 5, 2023, doi: 10.1145/3633453.

[20] Ravi Chandra Thota, "Enhancing resilience in cloud native architectures using well architected principles," *World J. Adv. Eng. Technol. Sci.*, vol. 1, no. 1, pp. 148–155, Dec. 2020, doi: 10.30574/wjaets.2020.1.1.0009.

[21] P. Vaithilingam, T. Zhang, and E. L. Glassman, "Expectation vs. experience: Evaluating code generation tools powered by LLMs," 2022.

[22] E. Frank and O. Godwin, "Enhancing Developer Productivity: a Study on GitHub Copilot's Code Completion Capabilities," Enhancing Developer Productivity: a Study on GitHub Copilot's Code Completion Capabilities. Accessed: Dec. 15, 2025. [Online]. Available: https://easychair.org/publications/preprint/5t9H

[23] R. L. Mesquita, G. M. Almeida, and P. G. de A. Barbosa, "Architectural technical debt identification in microservices: a systematic literature review," 2022.

[24] J. Ghofrani and D. Lubke, "Challenges of microservices architecture: A survey on the state of the practice," in *Challenges of Microservices Architecture: A Survey on the State of the Practice*, in CEUR workshop proceedings, vol. 2072. Dersden, Germany: CEUR workshop proceedings, 2018, p. 8. doi: Not%20official.

[25] P. Vaithilingam, T. Zhang, and E. L. Glassman, "Expectation vs. experience: Evaluating code generation tools powered by large language models," in *Extended Abstracts of the 2022 CHI Conference on Human Factors in Computing Systems*, in NA, vol. Not separate. USA: Association for computing machinery., 2022, p. 7. doi: 10.1145/3491101.3519665.

[26] Saurabh Kansal and Vanitha Sivasankaran Balasubramaniam, "Microservices Architecture in Large-Scale Distributed Systems: Performance and Efficiency Gains," 2024, *Unpublished*. doi: 10.13140/RG.2.2.36596.67202.

[27] N. Forsgren, J. Humble, and G. Kim, *The Science of Lean Software and DevOps; Building and Scaling High Performing Technology Organizations*, First., vol. 1, 1 vols. in NA, no. NA, vol. 1. USA: IT Revolution Press, 2018. Accessed: Dec. 15, 2025. [Online]. Available: https://itrevolution.com/book/accelerate/

[28] Gartner, "Cloud-Native Platforms: The Foundation of Modern CIO Strategy," *Gart. Res. Rep.*, vol. NA, no. NA, p. 19, 2023, doi: None.

[29] M. Richards, *Software Architecture Patterns for Composability and Modularity*. O'Reilly Media, 2022.

[30] National Institute of Standards and Technology (NIST), "Zero Trust Architecture," 2020.

[31] I. Seeber *et al.*, "Machines as teammates: A research agenda on AI in team collaboration," *Inf. Manage.*, vol. 57, no. 2, p. 22, 2019, doi: 10.1016/j.im.2019.103174.

[32] "Platform Engineering: Empowering Developers with Internal Developer Platforms (IDPs)," *Int. J. AI BigData Comput. Manag. Stud.*, vol. 5, 2024, doi: 10.63282/3050-9416.IJAIBDCMS-V5I1P110.

[33] S. Peng, E. Kalliamvakou, P. Cihon, and M. Demirer, "The impact of AI on developer productivity: Evidence from GitHub Copilot," *arXiv*, vol. NA, no. NA, p. 19, 2023, doi: arXiv:2302.06590.

[34] A. E. Viteri and D. Mauricio, "Artificial Intelligence in Software Testing: A Systematic Review of a Decade of Evolution and Taxonomy," *Algorithms*, vol. 18, no. 11, p. 64, 2025, doi: 10.3390/a18110717.

[35] Y. Remil, A. Bendimerad, R. Mathonat, and M. Kaytoue, "AIOps Solutions for Incident Management: Technical Guidelines and A Comprehensive Literature Review," 2024, *arXiv*. doi: 10.48550/ARXIV.2404.01363.

[36] Platform Engineering Org, "State of Platform Engineering Report," Platform Engineering Org, U.S, Industry research report volume 3, 2025. Accessed: Dec. 15, 2025. [Online]. Available: https://5890440.fs1.hubspotusercontent-eu1.net/hubfs/5890440/State%20of%20Platform%20Engineering%20Vol%204%202025.pdf?utm_source=chatgpt.com

[37] Y. Remil, A. Bendimerad, R. Mathonat, and M. Kaytoue, "AIOps solutions for incident management: technical guidelines and a comprehensive literature review," *arXiv*, vol. NA, no. NA, p. 82, 2024, doi: 10.48550/arXiv.2404.01363.

[38] Gartner, "Market Guide for Internal Developer Portals," Market Guide for Internal Developer Portals. Accessed: Dec. 15, 2025. [Online]. Available:
https://www.gartner.com/en/documents/4764631

[39] T. R. Velpucharla, "The Impact of Generative AI on Modern Software Development; Revolutionizing the Development Lifecycle," *Int. J. Sci. Res. Comput. Sci. Eng. Inf. Technol.*, vol. 11, no. 1, p. 9, 2025, doi: https://doi.org/10.32628/CSEIT251112219.

[40] Platform Engineering Org, "Whose cognitive load is it anyway?," Whose cognitive load is it anyway? Accessed: Dec. 15, 2025. [Online]. Available: https://platformengineering.org/blog/cognitive-load

[41] Gartner, "The Gartner Market Guide for Internal Developer Portals and Internal Developer Platforms," The Gartner Market Guide for Internal Developer Portals and Internal Developer Platforms. Accessed: Dec. 15, 2025. [Online]. Available:
https://www.gartner.com/en/documents

[42] E. Drosopoulou, "Platform Engineering with Backstage: Build your Internal Developer Portal," Platform Engineering with Backstage: Build your Internal Developer Portal. Accessed: Dec. 15, 2025. [Online]. Available:
https://www.javacodegeeks.com/2025/06/platform-engineering-with-backstage-build-your-internal-developer-portal.html

[43] Spotify Engineering, "Backstage: An open platform for building developer portals," Backstage: An open platform for building developer portals. Accessed: Dec. 09, 2025. [Online]. Available:
https://backstage.io/?utm_source=chatgpt.com

[44] Humanitec, "Platform Reference Architectures for Internal Developer Platforms (AWS/Azure/GCP)," Platform Reference Architectures for Internal Developer Platforms (AWS/Azure/GCP). Accessed: Dec. 15, 2025. [Online]. Available:

https://humanitec.com/reference-architectures

[45] PlatformEngineering.org, “Enterprise-grade Internal Developer Platform with Humanitec and Cortex,” Enterprise-grade Internal Developer Platform with Humanitec and Cortex. Accessed: Dec. 15, 2025. [Online]. Available: https://platformengineering.org/events/enterprise-grade-internal-developer-platform-with-humanitec-and-cortex?utm_source=chatgpt.com

[46] IBM Security, “Cost of a Data Breach Report 2023,” IBM Security, Armonk, NY, USA, Annual industry research report None published, 2023. Accessed: Dec. 09, 2025. [Online]. Available: https://secure-iss.com/wp-content/uploads/2023/07/Cost-of-a-Data-Breach-Report-2023.pdf

[47] S. Kapdi, “How to reduce developer cognitive load with Platform Engineering,” How to reduce developer cognitive load with Platform Engineering. Accessed: Dec. 15, 2025. [Online]. Available: https://www.improwised.com/blog/reduce-developer-cognitive-load-platform-engineering/?utm_source=chatgpt.com

[48] Shravan Kumar Reddy Padur, “AI-Augmented Platform Engineering: Transforming Developer Experience Through Intelligent Automation and Self-Optimizing Internal Platforms,” Sep. 2022, doi: 10.5281/ZENODO.17679433.

[49] P. R. Nangi and C. K. R. N. Obannagari, “A Multi-Layered Zero-Trust–Driven Cybersecurity Framework Integrating Deep Learning and Automated Compliance for Heterogeneous Enterprise Clouds,” *Am. Int. J. Comput. Sci. Technol.*, vol. 6, pp. 14–27, 2024, doi: 10.63282/3117-5481/AIJCST-V6I4P102.

[50] H. Pearce, B. Ahmad, B. Tan, B. Dolan-Gavitt, and R. Karri, “Asleep at the Keyboard? Assessing the Security of GitHub Copilot’s Code Contributions,” 2021, *arXiv*. doi: 10.48550/ARXIV.2108.09293.

[51] Palo Alto Networks Unit 42, "2024 Cloud Threat Report," Palo Alto Networks, Santa clara, CA headquarters, Research report NA, 2024. Accessed: Dec. 26, 2025. [Online]. Available: https://start.paloaltonetworks.com/rs/531-OCS-018/images/4.13PM_unit42-cloud-threat-report-volume7-final.pdf

[52] J. Bosch, *Continuous Software Engineering*, First., vol. 1, 1 vols. in Regular book, no. NA, vol. 1. Cham, Switzerland: Springer, 2014. Accessed: Dec. 09, 2025. [Online]. Available: https://link.springer.com/book/10.1007/978-3-319-11283-1

[53] G. Next and E. Kalliamvakou, "Research: Quantifying GitHub Copilot's Impact on Developer Productivity and Happiness," Research: Quantifying GitHub Copilot's Impact on Developer Productivity and Happiness. Accessed: Dec. 15, 2025. [Online]. Available: https://github.blog/news-insights/research/research-quantifying-github-copilots-impact-on-developer-productivity-and-happiness/

[54] D. G. Paul, H. Zhu, and L. Bayley, "Benchmarks and Metrics for Evaluations of Code Generation: A Critical Review," *Conf. Proc.*, vol. 390, no. NA, p. 8, 2024, doi: 10.1109/AITest62860.2024.00019.

[55] Escalante and David Mauricio, "Arificial intelligence in software testing: a systematic review of a decade of evolution and taxonomy," *Algorithms*, vol. 18, no. 11, p. 64, 2023, doi: 10.3390/a18110717.

[56] S. R. Cavalcante, E. R. Ribeiro, and A. Oran, "The Impact of AI Tools on Software Development; A Case Study with GitHub Copilot and Other AI Assistants," in *Proceedings of the 27th International Conference on Enterprise Information Systems*, in Proceedings of ICEIS, vol. 2. Europe: INSTICC, 2025, p. 252. doi: 10.5220/0013294700003929.

[57] D. Alahmadi, M. Alshangiti, and T. Alsubhi, "Source code classification based on generative pre-trained transformers," *Mathematics*, vol. 12, no. 13, p. 12, 2024, doi: 10.3390/math12132128.

[58] D. Drori and Y. Maarek, "Prompt Engineering for Large Language Models: A Survey," 2024.

[59] H. Pearce, B. Tan, B. ahmad, R. Karri, and B. Dolan-Gavitt, “Examining Zero-Shot Vulnerability Repair with Large Language Models,” in *2023 IEEE Symposium on security and privacy*, in IEEE Symposium on security and privacy, vol. NA. San Francisco: IEEE, 2023, p. 18. doi: 10.1109/SP46215.2023.10179324.
[60] D. Gondocs, S. Horvath, and V. Dorfler, “Uncovering the dynamics of human-AI hybrid performance: a qualitative review of empirical AI studies,” *Int. J. Human-Computer Stud.*, vol. 205, no. NA, p. 26, 2025, doi: 10.1016/j.ijhcs.2025.103622.
[61] T. M and D. U. Ramamoorthy, “AI-Driven Code Refactoring Assistant Using Large Language Models,” *Int. J. Sci. Innov. Eng.*, vol. 2, no. 9, p. 8, 2025, doi: https://doi.org/10.70849/IJSCI.
[62] M. Skelton and M. Pais, *Team Topologies: Organizing Business and Technology Teams for Fast Flow*, First., vol. 1, 1 vols. in NA, no. NA, vol. 1. USA: IT Revolution Press, 2019. Accessed: Dec. 09, 2025. [Online]. Available: https://teamtopologies.com/book?utm
[63] J. Bosch, “Speed, Data, and Ecosystems: The Future of Software Engineering,” *IEEE Softw.*, vol. 33, no. 1, p. 7, 2016, doi: 10.1109/MS.2016.14.
[64] J. Wei, “Chain-of-Thought Prompting Elicits Reasoning in Large Language Models,” *Adv. Neural Inf. Process. Syst. 35*, vol. 35, no. NA, p. 43, 2022, doi: 10.48550/arXiv.2201.11903.
[65] J. Bosch, “Speed, Data, and Ecosystems: The Future of Software Engineering,” *IEEE Softw.*, 2020.
[66] Akshay Nagpal *et al.*, “Framework for automating compliance verification in CI/CD pipelines,” Dec. 2024, doi: 10.5281/ZENODO.14259679.
[67] European Commission, “AI Act: Regulatory Framework for Trustworthy AI,” European Commission, Brussels, Belgium, EU Regulation Regulation (EU) 2024/1689, 2024. Accessed: Dec. 09, 2025. [Online]. Available:
https://assets.contentstack.io/v3/assets/blt3de4d56151f717f2/bltdcbb64d7c8139417/EU%20AI%20Act%20-%20%20English%20German.pdf

About the Author

Christopher Harasty is the Founder and Director of Harasty Consulting, a firm focused on helping organisations design, build, and scale high-performance technology solutions. With a background spanning enterprise systems, software development strategy, and digital transformation, Chris works at the intersection of business leadership and the implementation of advanced technology. He partners with executives and technical teams to modernise platforms, improve delivery capability, and unlock measurable business value through software.

Chris brings a pragmatic, commercially grounded perspective to enterprise technology. His work centres on aligning architecture, engineering practices, and organisational design to enable sustainable innovation. He has advised organisations across industries on system modernisation, data strategy, and the practical adoption of emerging technologies.

He is currently halfway through a PhD in Artificial Intelligence, where his research focuses on large language models (LLMs) and their application in enterprise environments. His academic work explores how advanced AI systems can be responsibly integrated into complex organisations to enhance decision-making, automation, and knowledge work.

Through his consulting, research, and writing, Chris is dedicated to shaping the future of enterprise software development—bridging rigorous technical insight with real-world execution.

Made in the USA
Monee, IL
14 September 2026

63198309R00115